Richaud 1993

ALCOHOL, TOBACCO AND DRUGS
Their Use and Abuse

W. WAYNE WORICK

Chicago State University

WARREN E. SCHALLER

Ball State University

PRENTICE-HALL, INC., *Englewood Cliffs, New Jersey 07632*

Library of Congress Cataloging in Publication Data

Worick, W.   Wayne, date
  Alcohol, tobacco, and drugs, their use and abuse.

  Includes index.
  1. Drug abuse.   2. Tobacco habit.   3. Temperance.
I. Schaller, Warren Edward, joint author.   II. Title.
HV5801.W68   362.2'9   76-30295
ISBN 0-13-021444-2
ISBN 0-13-021436-1 pbk.

Printed in the United States of America

10   9   8   7   6   5   4   3   2   1

PRENTICE-HALL INTERNATIONAL, INC., *London*
PRENTICE-HALL OF AUSTRALIA PTY. LIMITED, *Sydney*
PRENTICE-HALL OF CANADA, LTD., *Toronto*
PRENTICE-HALL OF INDIA PRIVATE LIMITED, *New Delhi*
PRENTICE-HALL OF JAPAN, INC., *Tokyo*
PRENTICE-HALL OF SOUTHEAST ASIA PTE. LTD., *Singapore*
WHITEHALL BOOKS LIMITED, *Wellington, New Zealand*

CONTENTS

Preface   v

one   Social Implications of the Use and Abuse
          of Alcohol, Tobacco and Drugs   1

          What is drug abuse?   2
          Effects of drug use and abuse on individuals   4
          Effects of drug abuse on society   6
          Effects on the family unit   9
          Summary   10

two   Theories on Drug Dependence   12

          Definition of key terms   13
          Psychological theories   16
          Sociological theories   20
          Hereditary or genetic theories   22
          Summary   22

three Alcohol   25

          Alcoholic beverages   26
          Alcohol and the economy   30
          Rates of alcohol consumption   32
          Patterns of alcohol use   40
          Metabolism of alcohol   42

Contents

Blood alcohol concentration   44
Effects on the central nervous system   48
Effects on sensory perception   54
Effects on emotions   54
Alcoholism and alcohol abuse   55
The stages of alcoholism   59
Alcohol related disorders   64
Treatment of alcoholism   68
Summary   72

four   Smoking and Health   77

Effects of smoking on the human body   78
Smoking statistics   88
Smoking and cancer   90
Smoking and cardiovascular disease   95
Smoking and respiratory diseases   98
Smoking and pregnancy   100
The psychology of smoking   101
Smoking cessation   104
Summary   106

five   Drug Use and Abuse   110

Legal drugs   110
Illegal drugs   113
Classification of drugs   115
Characteristics of drug abusers   125
U.S. studies   127
Summary   131

six   Countermeasures Against Alcohol, Tobacco and Drug Abuse   135

Alcohol countermeasures   135
Tobacco countermeasures   140
Drug abuse countermeasures   150
Summary   162

Index   166

PREFACE

Alcohol, Tobacco and Drugs: Their Use and Abuse is designed primarily for use in college-level courses. However, front-line workers in alcohol, tobacco and drug abuse programs, as well as high school teachers and administrators, may find the book a useful addition to their libraries. The book discusses the social and individual implications of alcohol, tobacco and drug use and abuse. An innovative separate chapter on theories on dependence is presented to broaden the perspectives of the reader and to help the reader understand some of the basic problems in the field. Present and potential new countermeasure programs are presented and evaluated.

The book recognizes that there are many reasons why people use and abuse alcohol, tobacco and drugs. When the right set of factors are present—e.g., cultural factors, drugs themselves and individual predisposition—the stage may be set for development of serious alcohol, tobacco and drug dependence. Countermeasure programs must deal with all these factors to be successful.

The central theme is that alcohol, tobacco and drugs are a part of our society and that our failure to deal with the resultant problems represents a betrayal to society. The book stresses education and prevention as the ultimate answer but recognizes that our present rehabilitation and enforcement programs must be expanded, upgraded and utilized if we are to reclaim those members of society that have been debilitated or lost through alcohol, tobacco and drug abuse. Also, our efforts at prevention and rehabilitation must be multidisciplined to be successful. Although existing laws are sufficient, it is clear that these laws must be fully utilized by our judiciary systems. They will be utilized if the public demands it.

It is incumbent upon professionals and lay persons alike to use all the resources available to stop the insidious spiral of abuse that has occurred in the last several decades. Relevant and creative educational programs, innovative rehabilitation programs and a full use of existing laws are needed. Let's do it!

All textbooks require contributions from many sources and this one is no exception. A special thanks to the following individuals who made such valuable contributions to this book: Dr. Charles R. Carroll, Professor, Department of Physiology and Health Science, Ball State University; Dr. Frank A. Wrestler, Assistant Professor, Department of Physiology and Health Science, Ball State University; Dr. Gerald Butler, Professor and Chairman, Department of Health, Physical Education and Recreation, Chicago State University; Mr. Sidney Miller, Associate Professor, Department of Health, Physical Education and Recreation, Chicago State University; Dr. David Rogers, Coordinator of Graduate Studies, Department of Health, Physical Education and Recreation, Chicago State University; and Ms. Marion Taylor, Associate Professor and Chairman, Department of Library Science, Chicago State University.

Much appreciation is extended to Mr. Walter Welch for his wise advice, counsel and understanding during the preparation of this book. Special thanks must be expressed to Mrs. Jane Jackson for the careful and accurate manner in which she typed the original manuscript.

Finally, it is our sincere hope that this book will help individuals develop a rational approach to the use of alcohol, tobacco and drugs.

W. Wayne Worick

Warren E. Schaller

one

SOCIAL IMPLICATIONS OF THE USE AND ABUSE OF DRUGS

Drugs are substances that cause changes in body function, and in this book we shall discuss those commonly used and misused. Drugs come in a wide variety of forms and have an even wider variety of uses. Drugs are found in nature, in our foods, and in chemical compositions made by man. Many drugs are consumed without any perceptible effects while others take a devastating toll, especially when abused. Some are socially acceptable and beneficial, some are not. The amount of public exposure to drugs overwhelms the imagination. They are sold by prescription, over the counter and through machines without medical advice, in legalized establishments, and through illegal markets on the streets.

Fortunately for mankind, most drugs do have a beneficial effect. Through the years a series of biological discoveries has produced an array of drugs that have had a profound effect on society. They have played a major role in providing comfort, curing disease, and extending the life span of mankind. We have witnessed, thanks to some of these discoveries, the almost complete control of diseases such as poliomyelitis, diphtheria, and smallpox, and an extension of the average length of life in the United States from 29 years in colonial times to over 70 years today.

The list of medical discoveries is long and impressive, beginning with the first vaccines and extending through the discovery of today's miracle drugs, tranquilizers and convenience drugs. (Birth

1

control pills are an example of a convenience drug.) We can reasonably expect this pharmacological revolution to continue with further benefits for mankind. We may even some day produce drugs which will increase mental ability.

However, the discovery and use of drugs has not been all good. Without question, the use and abuse of drugs such as alcohol, nicotine, cocaine and heroin, are having a pervasive negative impact on society by prematurely terminating the lives of many people, especially the young. For example, the lifespan of mankind is shortened by the thousands of premature deaths per year from alcohol-related diseases and accidents, from lung cancer and other respiratory diseases attributable to smoking, and from the self-destruction of our young by drug overdoses. Every time a person in the 18–24 age group dies, it has a greater effect on the average length of life than the death of a person who is near the end of the normal life span. Also affecting the average length of life are those who destroy themselves more slowly but still prematurely by the "preventable" affliction of drug abuse. Aside from the human misery and economic cost, this unnecessary loss of human resources is a sad commentary on our society.

WHAT IS DRUG ABUSE?

Drug abuse is hard to describe because it comes in many forms and manifests itself in many ways with varying effects upon society. Medically useful drugs can be improperly used, as well as drugs that have no legitimate medical application.

Anyone who uses a medically useful drug for a purpose other than that for which it was originally prescribed is abusing drugs. This type of drug abuse is very common, and includes the misuse of tranquilizers and infection-fighting drugs. For example, a college student may use an otherwise medically useful stimulant to stay awake while studying for an exam, or a housewife might take penicillin for a cold when it was originally prescribed for some other purpose. Both are abusing drugs.

One of the big dangers of self-diagnosis and self-medication is a delay in treatment for what may be a serious condition. In addition, the drug or drugs used may often appear to help but in fact may be dangerous and agitating to the condition over a period of time.

Remember, he who has himself for a doctor has a fool for a patient. At the same time, the medical doctor who indiscriminately gives prescriptions is promoting the abuse of drugs. Today we are witnessing widespread use of drugs such as LSD, heroin and marijuana. All these drugs are illegally produced and marketed. With the exception of LSD or marijuana used in a medically approved research program, anyone who uses them is abusing drugs. Popping morning glory seeds and injecting peanut butter into the veins are other types of drug abuse.

Often drug abuse takes the form of inhalation of fumes from gasoline, hair sprays, household cements, model airplane glue, and other chemicals. These have the ability to produce mood and behavior changes.

Some drugs are widely marketed on a legal basis without prescription and are socially acceptable today—for example, aspirin, alcohol, and the nicotine and tars of tobacco smoke. Ironically, these same drugs are some of the most commonly abused. The abuse of alcohol and tobacco alone has a devastating effect on society. The problem of drug abuse extends far beyond these few examples we have mentioned. In no instance does the drug abuser benefit.

Legislative efforts to curb drug abuse are not new. However, in recent years this legislation has been stepped up, and although many new agencies have been formed to intensify the fight against drug abuse, these efforts obviously are not sufficient. It is virtually impossible to effectively patrol our borders and to penetrate the underworld organizations responsible for the procurement and distribution of illegal drugs. Lack of cooperation among some producing countries is also a factor. It should be pointed out that the efforts of the various drug enforcement agencies are having an effect, as witnessed by the fact that heroin is becoming more scarce and more expensive on the streets. Also, the quality has supposedly degenerated.

Many medically useful drugs such as barbiturates and amphetamines are manufactured on a large scale. The widespread manufacturing and distribution of these drugs presents major problems because of the increased opportunities for illegal diversion, and because of legal diversion through prescription by some in the medical community. In Chapter 6 (Countermeasures Against Alcohol, Tobacco and Drug Abuse) you will find a brief review of the legislation against drug abuse.

As we will continue to stress, the best defense against drug abuse lies in education and enforcement. No new laws are needed. However, the inconsistency of present controls needs to be examined. Our schools represent the best place for effective education; they must step up their drug education programs. Present methods of education against drug abuse in our schools should be reexamined to make sure the programs are really effective, since there is some evidence that some drug education efforts have actually increased drug use and abuse. Since social pressures and environment apparently play such an important role in drug abuse, people must understand the implications of safe and unsafe drug-taking behavior. To date, we have let the horse out of the barn, so to speak; instead of educating to prevent drug abuse, we have focused on rehabilitation. Even then, efforts at rehabilitation have traditionally been assigned low priority.

EFFECTS OF DRUG USE AND ABUSE ON INDIVIDUALS

Whether or not to use drugs is an individual value judgment, and every individual should ask two questions when faced with this decision. They are:

1. What is the risk potential?
2. What are the possible benefits?

Both risk potential and benefits vary with the substance being considered and how it is to be used. Even the setting or "culture" in which a drug is taken may have a tremendous effect on the amount of risk involved. This is a systems approach to drug use. The individual must consider himself and others, he must consider the drug itself and he must consider the setting or environment in which the drug is to be used. See Figure 1-1.

Drugs with medicinal value taken under medical supervision generally carry a very low risk potential. However, it should be pointed out that even some of these drugs can be lethal if taken without medical supervision. Usually the advantages of taking drugs under medical supervision far outweigh the disadvantages. The decision-making process is often agitated by the fact that many drugs

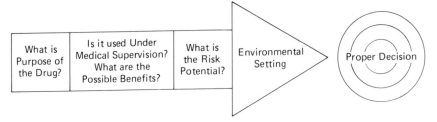

FIG. 1-1   The Value Judgment

are highly advertised and are legally and illegally obtained without prescription.

Alcohol is an example of a drug that is highly advertised, is available both legally and illegally, and can be used at the individual's own discretion. Actually, the benefits may be many to the user of alcohol. For example, it may be relaxing, increase sociability and, for some, carry a *low risk* potential. For others it may excite, decrease sociability, do bodily harm and have a *high risk* potential.

The point is that the individual alone must make the decision of whether to use a given drug. Except by physical compulsion, no one can force another person to take a drug. At the same time, except by physical restraint, no one can stop another individual from taking a drug.

The individual must then make a value judgment involving a *risk potential*. The ability to make this decision and still maintain a low risk potential will depend on such things as personal stability, the individual's sense of values and the information available to make the decision. For example, a person might choose not to drink based on a belief that just one drink could cause permanent damage (not a valid premise), or he or she might make the same decision based on a religious belief (a valid premise). A sound decision must be based on values that are relevant, logical, feasible and significant both for the individual and others.[1]

Proper drug use requires valid information regarding the drug and its effects. All too often an individual makes a decision regarding drug use that is based on a variety of misconceptions. Because of a decision based on false information, the individual may later become trapped or hooked in a situation of *drug abuse* with which he or she cannot cope. He or she may have crossed the fine line from simple drug abuse to drug dependence, either psychologically or physically, or possibly both.

Depending on the drug and its particular characteristics, the individual may be on a road to actual self-destruction. This can manifest itself with a decompensating effect on personal health, on ability to function and on dealings with others. The ultimate effects may be premature death or permanent disability, disintegration of the family or social unit and an adverse effect on the community as a whole.

The individual economic cost of narcotic addiction is staggering. The following figures are only estimates and they change very rapidly. The average narcotic addict spends approximately $58 per day on his habit. This goes on day after day without suspension. This person, over a brief period of one year, will spend over $21,000 on his habit.[2] Some addicts spend over $200 a day on their habit.[3] Think what a person, if not very wealthy, must do to support such a habit.

The same financial problems may arise from other forms of drug abuse. In the case of tobacco, if a person smokes two packs of cigarettes a day the cost is roughly $1 per day. Let's assume the individual starts smoking at age 15 and smokes until age 60. Had this $1 per day been deposited in a savings account bearing 6 percent interest, the individual would have accumulated approximately $83,000 over the 45 years. People worry about the high price of foods and at the same time pay $15 a pound for cigarettes.

Drug abuse has the potential to extract a high personal price, both physically and financially, a price that even the most healthy and wealthy can ill-afford. Therefore, every individual owes it to himself and to society to refrain from drug abuse.

EFFECTS OF DRUG ABUSE ON SOCIETY

In recent years, drug abuse has become a national health crisis crossing all strata of society. It occurs in all social and economic classes. Alcoholism alone ranks among the major national health threats, along with cancer, heart disease and mental illness.

The actual extent of drug abuse is unknown. For statistical information we are heavily dependent on the records of police departments, hospital emergency rooms, and treatment and rehabilitation centers. Obviously, thousands of drug-dependent people and other drug abusers never come in contact with these agencies; therefore, these figures are only indicators of the severity of the problem.

For example, estimates concerning the incidence of alcoholism range from 4 to 9 million persons. There are millions more problem drinkers and heavy drinkers. The fact that we do not have clear lines of delineation between an alcoholic, a problem drinker, a heavy drinker or even a social drinker, makes the problem of obtaining accurate statistical information virtually impossible.

In order to further illustrate the confusion centering around the extent of drug abuse in this country, let's examine the tremendous variations in estimates of narcotics abuse. The Drug Enforcement Administration reports that some 95,879 active narcotic addicts were recorded as of June 30, 1973. This represents about 1 addict for every 2170 people. They further state that as of June 30, 1973, a more realistic estimate might be 612,478 narcotic addicts.[4] One must admit this represents a wide variation in estimated incidence.

They further report that most of the addicts are from seven states. New York accounts for over 51 percent of the narcotic addicts. This figure goes up to over 80 percent with the addition of New Jersey, California, Illinois, Florida, Pennsylvania and Michigan. They also report that about 70 percent of these addicts are between ages 18 and 30.[5]

These figures pertain only to narcotic abuse. They do not include estimates of the use and abuses of nonnarcotic drugs such as marijuana, hallucinogens, stimulants and depressants. Studies concerning the use of marijuana at different schools and colleges show the extent of use may vary from 0 to 69 percent. Based on projections from some of these studies, a Federal health agency estimates that 12 to 20 million persons in the United States have tried marijuana at least once. (One-time use of marijuana should not necessarily be considered a serious form of drug abuse.) Lower percents are reported for LSD, amphetamines, and barbiturates. Surveys of junior high and elementary schools are still fragmentary, but observers mention that drug use is increasing among younger children.[6] The exposure of our elementary school children to illicit drug traffic is alarming. It is here that the drug abuse problem could have the most devastating effect upon society by affecting our most valuable natural resource.

There are tremendous economic implications in drug abuse for society. To illustrate this, let's first consider the cost of heroin (a narcotic) addiction. As we mentioned earlier, the average heroin addict spends $58 a day on his habit. Based on these estimates, the cost of heroin for addicts in the United States is $36.3 million per day or $13.2 billion per year.[7] If the drug-dependent person turns to stealing to support his habit (a common approach), he must secure approximately $3 to $5 in stolen goods to produce $1 in cash. Just to support a $58 per day habit he must steal approximately $200 worth of property per day. This amounts to $73,000 a year.[8]

Obviously, some drug-dependent people do work, and others may sell drugs to support their habit. But if we use a figure of 60 percent of the estimated 600,000 drug-dependent people as stealing to support their habit, the cost is approximately $27 billion a year in stolen property.[9] We should further realize that much of this money goes into the underworld where it is used to support illegal activities. Also, society picks up the tab for rehabilitation of the addict. If we had treatment programs for all heroin addicts, the cost of this alone would run into billions more. Even today, we are spending billions in rehabilitation centers and treatment programs for the various types of drug abusers as an ill-prepared society tries to reclaim its members.

In the case of alcohol consider the following fact: alcohol abuse and alcoholism drain the economy of an estimated $15 billion a year.[10] Ten billion of this is due to work loss in industry, civilian government and the military. Two billion is spent for health and welfare services to alcoholics and their families. Property damages, medical expenses and other overhead costs take a toll of 3 billion or more.[11]

Public intoxication accounts for approximately one-third of all arrests annually. If you include such alcohol-related offenses as driving under the influence, disorderly conduct and vagrancy, this figure rises to between 40 and 49 percent.[12] Think of the costs to the taxpaying public for these arrests and for maintaining jails which to a large extent are necessary to accommodate people committing alcohol-related offenses. The dissipation of police energies which otherwise could be spent in more valuable ways is also a serious problem.

Approximately one-half of all highway fatalities are alcohol-related either directly or indirectly. This took almost 28,000 lives in a recent year. Half of all homicides and one-third of all suicides are alcohol-related, accounting for about 11,700 deaths per year.[13]

These statistics do not tell the full story of drug abuse. They neglect the human misery, the broken homes, the resultant shorter lifespan of mankind and the loss of valuable services to society because the individual cannot function to full capacity.

Despite all the evidence, we are still a nation with mixed emotions concerning drug use and abuse. Many of our current attitudes are built around folklore concerning drugs. This folklore is built on both fact and fiction. We tend to discourage drug use for other than medical reasons and at the same time encourage drug use through cocktail hours, cocktail parties, pot parties, smoking breaks, etc. In the case of alcohol, we drink to calm down, we drink to stimulate ourselves after a hard day, we drink to create an appetite and then we drink to help digest a heavy meal. We drink to cool off, to warm up, to sleep, to stay awake and for a host of other reasons.

Dr. Morris E. Chafetz, former Director of the National Institute on Alcohol Abuse and Alcoholism described America's ambivalence concerning drugs this way:

> While we agonize over the possibility that our children might join the ranks of the Nation's quarter of a million hard drug addicts, we pay scant attention to the possibility that they stand a far better chance of joining the Nation's nine million alcoholic and problem drinkers. Non-alcoholic drugs are somehow foreign and frightening, because their use, except as medicine, is not yet accepted as part of the mainstream of American culture. Alcohol, on the other hand, is so common a drug that we tend to ignore it—and its victims—as we have done for far too long[14]

EFFECTS ON THE FAMILY UNIT

The effects of drug abuse on the family unit, in the end, may prove to be the most disastrous. The family unit is the most basic unit in this country. We have family units, township units, city units, county units, state units and finally the Federal government. We are a structured society.

Theoretically, destruction of the family unit could ultimately cause our society to fall, because this small unit provides the basic foundation for our entire society. Drug abuse affects the family unit in many ways. The fact that divorce rates continue to rise is due in some small part to drug abuse. It is an established fact that alcohol abuse alone is having a devastating effect on the preservation of the family unit.

Today we are seeing children born who are addicted to alcohol (Fetal Alcohol Syndrome). In some cases they suffer from liver damage at birth and manifest withdrawal symptoms. We are recognizing functional abnormalities, as well as structural abnormalities and lower IQ's, among the offspring of women who are heavy drinkers. Children born to heroin-addict mothers are often addicted at birth.

Pregnant women who smoke have a greater number of still-births than nonsmoking women, and their infants are more likely to die in the first month. Their babies often weigh less than five and one-half pounds. This is considered premature and the babies are more vulnerable to disease and death.[15]

Children born into families where drug abuse is prevalent are denied clothing, education and food. Many families barely survive because of the spendable income dissipated through drug abuse. The resulting financial hardships, human misery, and psychological ramifications strangle the most basic unit in society, the family. Should the family unit disintegrate, as it inevitably does under these circumstances, then society picks up the tab in added welfare and rehabilitation costs. It is impossible to accurately estimate this cost.

SUMMARY

Although drugs provide many benefits to mankind and will continue to do so, the abuse of drugs is counteracting many of these benefits. Thus our drug use has become a paradox. We are supposedly a sophisticated society with an abundance of technological knowledge. At the same time we allow alcohol, tobacco and drug abuse to continue making serious inroads into our ability to make further progress and possibly even to survive.

Without question, the abuse of all drugs—including alcohol, tobacco, narcotics and other stimulants and depressants—represents a malignancy upon our society. There is real irony in the fact that we spend more on alcohol, tobacco and drug abuse than on education, that there are probably more good bartenders than there are good health teachers, that, in effect, we actually strive to promote our own downfall.

BIBLIOGRAPHY (CHAPTER 1)

American Cancer Society, Inc., *Danger*, Pamphlet, n.d.

American Alliance for Health, Physical Education, and Recreation, *Learning about Alcohol*, ed. SAMUEL A. MILES. Washington, D.C., 1974.

CHAFETZ, MORRIS E., Foreword in *Facts about Alcohol and Alcoholism*, ed. LEONARD C. HALL. National Institute on Alcohol Abuse and Alcoholism, Department of Health Education and Welfare Publication No. (ADM) 74-31, Rockville, Md., 1974.

Department of Health, Education and Welfare, *First Report to Congress on Alcohol and Health*. Washington, D.C., 1971.

Drug Enforcement Administration, *Fact Sheets*. Washington, D.C., 1973.

National Institute on Alcohol Abuse and Alcoholism (DHEW), *Facts about Alcohol and Alcoholism*, ed. LEONARD C. HALL. Department of Health Education and Welfare Publication No. (ADM) 74-31, Rockville, Md., 1974.

National Institute on Alcohol Abuse and Alcoholism (DHEW), *Alcohol and Alcoholism, Problems, Programs, and Progress*. Washington, D.C., 1972.

FOOTNOTES (CHAPTER 1)

[1]American Alliance for Health, Physical Education, and Recreation, *Learning about Alcohol*, ed. Samuel A. Miles (Washington, D.C., 1974), p. 69.

[2]Drug Enforcement Administration, *Fact sheets* (Washington, D.C., 1973), p. 16.

[3]*Ibid.*

[4]*Ibid.*

[5]*Ibid.*

[6]*Ibid.*

[7]*Ibid.*

[8]*Ibid.*

[9]*Ibid.*

[10]U.S. Department of Health, Education and Welfare, *First Special Report to Congress on Alcohol and Health* (Washington, D.C., 1971), p. viii.

[11]*Ibid.*

[12]*Ibid.*

[13]National Institute on Alcohol Abuse and Alcoholism (DHEW), *Alcohol and Alcoholism, Problems, Programs and Progress* (Washington, D.C., 1972), p. 11.

[14]Morris E. Chafetz, Foreword in *Facts about Alcohol and Alcoholism*, ed. Leonard C. Hall (Rockville, Md.: National Institute of Alcohol Abuse and Alcoholism, 1974), p. iii.

[15]American Cancer Society, *Danger*, Pamphlet, n.d.

two

THEORIES ON DRUG DEPENDENCE

Drug dependence has disabled people all over the world for thousands of years. To date, no single theory has proven adequate to explain why certain individuals and groups succumb to drug dependence while others do not. The problem transcends the disciplines of psychology, sociology, physiology, medicine and others. Consequently there are as many theories regarding the predisposition for and causes of dependence as there are disciplines dealing with the problem, and it is appropriate that we briefly present several theories for your consideration. In all probability the answer lies in a combination of spiritual, psychological, sociological and physiological factors. This indicates the need for a multifaceted approach featuring close cooperation among various disciplines.

The development of proven theories on dependence has great implications for both the prevention and treatment of drug abuse and drug dependence. For example, if we could say, "A person who exhibits certain physical or emotional traits, if placed in a given environment, will in all probability develop a drug dependence," it would aid us in the development of prevention programs and techniques.

The understanding of the "Why" of drug abuse would have even greater implications in the development of treatment procedures since we could aim treatment directly at the root causes. The discovery of a method of developing animal models duplicating human characteristics of addiction would be a great leap forward. In this discussion much reference is placed on physiological addiction to alcohol. We do not necessarily intend to equate physiological and psychological dependence on alcohol to other drugs. Eventually scientific evidence may clearly delineate the etiological factors involved in the various types of drug dependence.

For example there are great differences in the numbers of users who become physiologically dependent on alcohol and heroin. Whereas about one in fifteen alcohol users becomes dependent upon alcohol, the number of heroin users who become physiologically dependent upon heroin is much, much higher. Also the time or duration of drug usage before the onset of physical dependence varies greatly from one type of drug to another. Physical dependence on some drugs develops slowly while physical dependence on others is very rapid, occurring within days or weeks. Also, the quantity of dosage required before physical dependence occurs varies from drug to drug.

Therefore one must recognize there are many variables in physical dependence. This fact plays a major role in the proliferation of theories as scientists research for definite answers. Our purpose here is to acquaint you with only a few of these theories and to broaden your understanding of the multitude of problems in the areas of drug use and abuse.

DEFINITION OF KEY TERMS

A glaring problem in dealing with drug use and abuse is that of definitions. Any discussion on the subject immediately brings up such terms as dependence, addiction, habituation, tolerance, etc. In fact, if one attends a seminar on drugs he will be dismayed at the amount of time spent trying to arrive at acceptable definitions of such terms. It is important in understanding discussions that you realize the context in which certain statements are made. For that reason we are presenting some key definitions at the outset. The World Health Organization's (WHO) Expert Committee on Addiction Producing Drugs has long recognized this problem. For example, in the committee's thirteenth report (1964) they recommended that the terms drug addiction and drug habituation be dropped in favor of a more precise term "drug dependence."[1] WHO defines *drug dependence* as follows:

> Drug dependence is a state of psychic or physical dependence, or both, on a drug, arising in a person following administration of that drug on a periodic or continuing basis. The characteristics of such state will vary with the agent involved, and these characteristics must always be made clear by designating the particular type of drug dependence in each specific case; for example, drug dependence of morphine type, of amphetamine type, etc.

The definition recognizes dependence as being of either a psychological or physical nature, or both. The definition also recognizes that dependence is of a variable nature depending on the agent or drug involved. For accuracy, the World Health Organization has classified the major types of drug dependence as follows:[2]

1. The morphine type
2. The barbiturate–alcohol type
3. The cocaine type
4. The cannabis (marijuana) type
5. The amphetamine type
6. The hallucinogen (LSD) type
7. The khat type

Despite the fact that the World Health Organization has recommended that the terms drug habituation and addiction be dropped, these terms are still widely used. In fact, they are preferred by some people. Because of this preference it is necessary to include these terms here. WHO defines *drug addiction* as a state of periodic

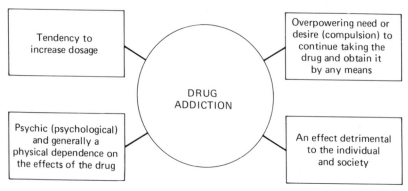

FIG. 2-1   Drug Addiction

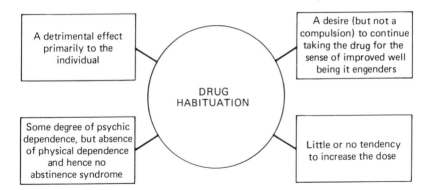

FIG. 2-2   Drug Habituation

or chronic intoxication produced by the repeated consumption of a drug, whether it be natural or synthetic, which produces specified characteristics. Figure 2-1 shows the characteristics of drug addiction as specified by the World Health Organization.

Drug habituation is a condition resulting from the repeated administration of a drug. Figure 2-2 shows the characteristics of drug habituation as specified by the World Health Organization.

Because several individual studies are cited in this book, you will find all the terms—dependence, habituation and addiction —used. However, we agree that the term *dependence* seems more reasonable and will use it as the common denominator whenever possible. Some other commonly used terms and suggested definitions are as follows:

1. **Drug abuse:** The persistent and excessive use of a drug beyond medical need.

2. **Tolerance:** The build up or cumulation of resistance to the effects of a drug. After tolerance builds up it takes heavier dosage to have the same effects. This is thought to be the basis for physiological dependence (see Abstinence Syndrome).

3. **Cross-tolerance:** Carryover of tolerance from one drug to another. This occurs among pharmacologically related drugs. Tolerance built up to the effects of one drug will carry over to the others. An example is methadone and heroin. If one has taken a large dose of methadone, heroin will have no perceivable effects. This is the basis of the methadone treatment.[3]

4. **Abstinence Syndrome:** Refers to the complex of symptoms which appear when one stops taking certain drugs. This is the result of physiological dependence which apparently occurs when the metabolic functions of the cells adapt to the presence of a drug on a

regular basis. Apparently, once cellular metabolic functions have been altered, removal of the drug causes a cellular "revolution" expressed as the withdrawal symptom. The withdrawal symptoms are different for different types of drugs. For example, anxiety, tremors, weakness, sweating, nausea, vomiting and diarrhea characterize the withdrawal symptoms in the case of alcohol. These may be accompanied by delirium tremens (DT's). The period of withdrawal is usually about one week. Medical treatment is essential during the withdrawal process since it can be and is often fatal.

Withdrawal from heroin is characterized by hot and cold flashes, watery eyes, running nose, vomiting, diarrhea, very painful muscle spasms and an increase in blood pressure, heart rate and breathing rate. These usually begin about 4–6 hours after the last fix, with the worst time being 18–24 hours after the symptoms begin. Although the withdrawal process may extend to one or two weeks, it is rarely fatal.

PSYCHOLOGICAL THEORIES:

Theorists in this area explain drug dependence as a symptom of some underlying personality or emotional disorder. There are three major types of psychological theories—the conditioned learning theory, the personality trait theory, and the psychoanalytic theory.

The Learning Theory

The conditioned learning theory is commonly chosen to explain drug abuse. The suggestion is made that the person becomes conditioned to internal and external stimuli which are similar for a variety of drugs. In other words, drug taking is explained as a reflex response to some stimulus and as a way of reducing inner drives such as fear and anxiety. This theory holds situations in terms of approach and avoidance. In other words, people tend to be drawn to pleasant situations and repelled from unpleasant situations. Further explanation of this theory might be as follows:

As one strives to solve his daily problems and attain the desired goals of life, he encounters problems or stumbling blocks (see Figure 2-3). These stumbling blocks vary in size and intensity, causing corresponding degrees of stress. These frustrations or stresses occur daily and the success a person enjoys in dealing with them is indicative of his ability to maintain a desirable balance in life's

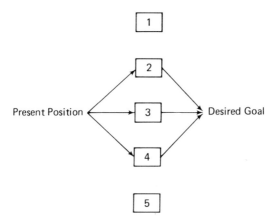

FIG. 2-3 Stumbling Blocks

activities. Inability to deal with these stresses and frustrations with reasonable success is indicative of an emotional disorder.

Frustrations and stresses affect emotions, resulting in mood swings. Figure 2-4 graphically illustrates these mood swings. The well-adjusted person tends to stay within certain limits, except perhaps for drastic situations such as the death of a loved one, etc.; however, many people chronically exhibit "highs" and "lows" that are so extreme they are considered abnormal.[4] During these mood swings they are subject to high accident rates, suicides and other psychological phenomena including excessive use of escape mechanisms.

The use of escape mechanisms, a normal reaction, helps us deal with frustrations and stresses. Escape mechanisms are healthy if properly used and not abused. It is when they begin to pervade all

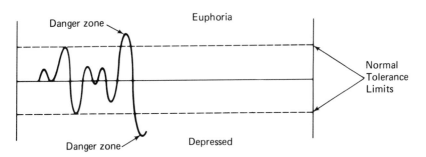

FIG. 2-4 Tolerance Limits

our normal activities that they become serious. For example, if a person watches television as an escape mechanism and fails to go to work, etc., then the escape mechanism has pervaded his normal routine. At this point, the use of the escape mechanism has become abnormal and perhaps dangerous. Fortunately, watching television is not physiologically addicting.

Unfortunately many drugs can also be used as escape mechanisms. When one uses drugs and finds relief and tranquility or some other desired result, a psychological dependence may develop. This psychological dependence itself is bad enough, but when coupled with the fact that certain drugs produce physiological or chemical dependence, the situation becomes especially dangerous.

Once the psychological dependence develops, the person may continue to use the drug, finding different degrees of satisfaction with each encounter. Any drug such as alcohol, for example, that has capabilities of producing physical or chemical dependence, if used long enough, can eventually "capture" the individual. This could be, in fact is, the point of no return for many individuals.

The avoidance aspects of the conditioned learning theory seem to be in conflict with what actually happens to some drug-dependent people. For example, why does the alcoholic or heroin addict continue to take the drug in the face of such consequences as loss of job, family, etc.? Apparently the physical dependence, which is not completely understood, renders the victim helpless. Some people supporting this theory might say that the guilt and anxiety arising from the consequences of the excessive drug ingestion may also induce another round of drug abuse. In fact, there are many questions raised regarding this theory, since there is not enough empirical evidence to understand the process of drug use, the types of drug users, and factors involved in drug action.

Personality Trait Theory

This theory is based on the premise that drug abusers exhibit certain personality traits or clusters of traits that should be detectable and should correlate with a predisposition to drug abuse. Much of this work has been done in the field of alcoholism, as theorists have long searched for an "alcoholic personality."

One of the major drawbacks in this type of theory is that

researchers must necessarily use drug abusers during the study as they identify traits and characteristics that are common to the group. For example, low frustration tolerance is a common finding. Now, how do you discern which caused which? Did the drug abuse cause the low frustration tolerance or did the low frustration tolerance trigger the drug abuse?

As one develops a list of traits and characteristics common to the group of drug abusers being studied, it often becomes evident that the list of traits is common to many groups suffering from different types of mental illness. Also, many of the individual traits are found in people who are functioning very well.

In the case of alcoholism, Howard T. Blane has listed some personality characteristics he feels appear often enough to warrant consideration in the treatment and rehabilitation. He recognizes that these traits are not present in all alcoholics. He further recognizes that these traits appear in nonalcoholics but they are not centrally important to the personality of the nonalcoholic.[5]

Blane lists the following characteristics as commonly appearing in alcoholics.[6]

1. Low frustration tolerance
2. Sociability
3. Feelings of inferiority combined with attitudes of superiority
4. Fearfulness
5. Dependency

It should be pointed out that researchers and theorists have for years attempted to explain certain cultural phenomena through personality traits. A classic example of this has been the attempts to identify personality traits common to those who are supposedly accident prone. Surprisingly enough, many of the characteristics found among the "accident prone" are found in Blane's list of characteristics commonly found among alcoholics.

A study on personality pathology among students using drugs, done at the University of Canterbury in New Zealand, found that there was no significant difference between the personality of the users and the nonusers of drugs. They feel that earlier studies have suffered a sampling bias.

Thirty-eight male drug users were selected by first conducting a survey to determine the number of users on campus, and then by a referral method which would give the proportion of drug users needed for the study. A control group of the same number of nonusers was secured. Both groups were given the Minnesota Multiphasic Personality Inventory. The drug users scored slightly lower on the validity scale and the psychopathic deviant scale, but the differences were not statistically significant. No difference was found in the frequency of occurrence of abnormal personality profiles between the drug-using and control groups.

The investigators felt that the type of student who now smokes marijuana has changed from a hippie type to a more conventional student. However, this does not account for the multidrug user who also showed little deviation from normal. They indicate that the type of study which they have done needs to be done by other researchers before their conclusion is fully accepted.[7]

Personality trait studies may have considerable value when related to treatment and treatment methods. However, to date we have not been able to effectively isolate personality traits common only to alcoholics, for example. This is not to say we should not continue efforts in this direction.

Psychoanalysis Theories

These theories usually assume that the person has been fixated at the oral level of psychosexual development. Supposedly, drugs release inhibitions of repressed urges relating to oral tendencies and latent homosexuality. Presumably these traits develop because of poor parent–child relationships, resulting in failure of the child to develop self control, fixing his development at the oral stage, leading to over-identification with the father. Inability to develop valid experimental tests for these theories tend to make them inconclusive.[8]

SOCIOLOGICAL THEORIES

Different cultures have different rates of drug use and abuse. Sociologists usually try to explain these differences by examining the values and attitudes of the various cultures. The most extensive research into the area of sociological differences in drug use and abuse has probably been directed at alcohol.

In the case of alcohol use and alcoholism we have seen some striking differences between social cultures. For example, high rates of alcoholism are reported among the northern French; Americans, especially Irish-Americans; American and Alaskan Indians; Swedes; Poles; Swiss; and northern Russians. Conversely, certain cultures show relatively low incidences of alcoholism. Examples are the Italians, some Chinese groups, Orthodox Jews, Greeks, Portuguese, Spaniards and southern French.[9]

Interestingly enough some of these groups exhibiting low incidences of alcoholism use alcohol rather extensively in their daily routines. The Italians use wine with their noon and evening meals. The Jewish people use alcohol in religious rituals.

Certain groups such as the Italians dilute the alcohol before serving it to youngsters at mealtime. Most groups with low rates of alcoholism tend to condemn excessive drinking. Apparently the members of the "low incidence" societies know and accept the attitudes of their society. Also, strong family and religious ties may be important factors in reducing alcoholism.

Undoubtedly, analysis of different rates of drug abuse in various groups will reveal many differences, since there are apparently several factors which contribute to drug use and abuse. Traditional moral standards which label drug use and abuse as bad or immoral have a bearing on drug use and abuse. These moral standards are often translated into laws, making the use and abuse of a drug either legal or illegal. Of course, society must accept these laws if they are to be successful. Today we are seeing our own society undergo the pains of indecision as we face the problem of how to handle the marijuana problem. Along with this ambivalent attitude toward marijuana and its control we are seeing an increase in the use of the drug, despite the fact that it is still technically illegal.

The particular level of society that is most severely affected by the problem has a lot to do with the attitude of the entire society. For example, now that heroin addiction has escaped the ghettos and reached into the sanctities of white suburbia, it has suddenly become a "serious problem" deserving the attention of all society.

When the history of today's drug use is finally written, we may find that our present systems of mass communication have played an important role. In years past we had considerable difficulty gaining public acceptance of a new drug or vaccine. Now, television and on-the-spot coverage show "instant" success in the use of drugs to many health problems. But this same communication system also serves to promote the use of dangerous drugs.

It does appear that ambivalent attitudes on the part of society toward drug use and abuse create confusion and increase the problem. As can be expected, societies having closely knit family units and strong religious ties tend not to have ambivalent attitudes toward drug use and abuse.

HEREDITARY OR GENETIC THEORIES

Genetic theories claim that a particular predisposition or condition leading to addiction is passed through genes from parent to offspring at the time of conception.

Some of these theories combine other factors, such as a genetic trait and a nutritional deficiency. For example, they postulate that an inherited trait such as defective metabolism would result in a nutritional deficiency. The resulting nutritional deficiency would then result in an unusual craving for a certain drug such as alcohol.

Alcoholism does occur in families. The fact that alcoholism occurs with high incidence among Indians could indicate heredity as a factor. The theory that some individuals cannot properly metabolize alcohol due to some enzyme deficiency could possibly be considered to be hereditary.

Although the possibility of genetic predisposition to addiction has not been ruled out, evidence proving or pointing to genetic predisposition is to date unsatisfactory.

SUMMARY

Scientists have postulated many theories regarding the cause of drug dependence. Present knowledge indicates that drug dependence begins for different reasons with different people. Thus no single theory will suffice to explain drug dependence. No common denominator seems to pervade all the different forms of drug dependence.

Many of these theories have sufficient evidence to be a cause for concern. For example, environment and societal attitudes must play an important role. Possibly, there are genetic and psychological predispositions that can cause drug dependence to develop. Characteristics specific to the drugs themselves may be important in determining causes of dependence. Whatever the actual reason, if the right set of circumstances is present certain individuals do readily develop drug dependence. Since the "certain circumstances" cut across many fields of study, a multidisciplined approach to the problems seems advisable.

BIBLIOGRAPHY (CHAPTER 2)

BLANE, HOWARD T., "The Personality of the Alcoholic," in MORRIS E.CHAFETZ, HOWARD T. BLANE and MARJORIE J. HILL., *Frontiers of Alcoholism*, ed. New York: Science House, 1970.

COHEN, SIDNEY, *The Drug Dilemma*. New York: McGraw-Hill, 1969.

Institute on Alcohol Abuse and Alcoholism (DHEW), *Alcohol and Alcoholism, Problems, Programs and Progresses*. Washington, D.C., 1972.

LINGEMAN, RICHARD R., *Drugs from A to Z*, 2nd ed. rev. New York: McGraw-Hill, 1974.

RILEY, D. N., and B. D. JAMIESON, "Personality, Pathology and Student Drug Use," *New Zealand Medical Journal* (Oct. 1972).

U. S. Department of Health, Education and Welfare, *First Special Report to the U.S. Congress on Alcohol and Health*, ed. MARK KELLER and SHIRLEY S. ROSENBERG, et al. Washington, D.C., 1971.

WORICK, W. WAYNE, *Safety Education: Man, His Machines and Environment*. Englewood Cliffs, N.J.: Prentice-Hall, 1975.

FOOTNOTES (CHAPTER 2)

[1]Richard R. Lingeman, *Drugs from A to Z*, 2nd ed. rev. (New York: McGraw;Hill, 1974), p. 64.

[2]Sidney Cohen, *The Drug Dilemma* (New York: McGraw-Hill, 1969), p. 7.

[3]Lingeman, *op. cit.*, p. 56.

[4]W. Wayne Worick, *Safety Education: Man, His Machines and Environment* (Englewood Cliffs, N.J.: Prentice-Hall, 1975), p. 37.

[5]Howard T. Blane, "The Personality of the Alcoholic," in *Frontiers of Alcoholism*, ed. Morris E. Chafetz,, Howard T. Blane and Marjorie J. Hill (New York: Science House, 1970), p. 16.

[6]*Ibid.*, pp. 16–28.

[7]D. N. Riley and B. D. Jamieson, "Personality, Pathology and Student Drug Use," *New Zealand Medical Journal* 76 (Oct. 1972), p. 252.

[8]U.S. Department of Health, Education and Welfare, *First Special Report to the U.S. Congress on Alcohol and Health*, ed. Mark Keller and Shirley S. Rosenberg, et al. (Washington, D.C., 1971), p. 64.

[9]Institute on Alcohol Abuse and Alcoholism (DHEW), *Alcohol and Alcoholism, Problems, Programs and Progress* (Washington, D.C., 1972), p. 15.

three

ALCOHOL

Alcohol comes in a variety of forms and is prepared in many different ways. Ethyl alcohol (ethanol) is used in alcoholic beverages. It is sometimes called *grain alcohol* and is the only type that is relatively safe for human consumption. The chemical formula for ethyl alcohol (ethanol) is C_2H_5OH; it is chemically similar to ether and like ether can be used as anesthetic. Methyl alcohol (wood alcohol) is commonly used in commercial products such as antifreezes and fuels. It is *unsafe* for human consumption since it cannot be metabolized properly by the body. Methyl alcohol is toxic and damages the optic nerves frequently resulting in blindness. Wood alcohol is occasionally found in illegal or "moonshine liquor," reason enough never to consume illegal whiskey. Isopropyl alcohol is another well-known alcohol; it is commonly used as a solvent, as a disinfectant and for massage purposes. It is sometimes called "rubbing alcohol," and it too is *unsafe* for human consumption.

Much research has been done on ethyl alcohol and its effects on the human body. Our discussion will be limited to ethyl (ethanol) alcohol since it is the only type safe for human consumption.

Ethyl alcohol is produced by fermentation, a chemical process that was probably discovered accidentally. Alcohol content or "proof" can be strengthened by a physical process called "distillation." Both of these processes are discussed later in this chapter. Alcohol content is one-half the proof rating. One hundred proof means 50 percent alcohol by volume, 80 proof means 40 percent alcohol and so on.

ALCOHOLIC BEVERAGES

There is evidence that man used ethyl alcohol in the form of wines as far back as 6000 B.C. Since then it has been used in cultures all over the world for different reasons, including religious rituals. Beer was transported to this country on the *Mayflower* and may have played a part in the decision of the Pilgrims to land at Plymouth Rock, instead of farther south as they had originally planned. A diary from the *Mayflower*, in an entry dated December 19, 1620, states that the landing at Plymouth was necessitated because "We could not now take time for further search or consideration: our victuals being much spent, especially our beere. . ." A copy of this diary, kept by one of the passengers, is in the Library of Congress.[1]

Had it not been for beer, then, some site other than Plymouth Rock might have been enshrined, and someone other than John Alden might have wooed Priscilla Mullins on behalf of Myles Standish. John, a cooper by trade, was on the Mayflower to take care of the beer barrels.[2]

The Massachusetts Bay Colony issued the first license to operate a brewery to Captain Robert Sedgwick in 1637. Probably the most famous of all brewers in early American history was Samuel Adams, "Father of the Revolution," who inherited a brewery from his father.[3] George Washington liked beer so well he had his own recipe, which is preserved in his handwriting at the New York Public Library. Thomas Jefferson went so far as to send to Bohemia for brewers who could teach the niceties of their art to Americans.[4] Similar evidence of the importance of beers and wine can be traced to other countries, such as England, Holland and Germany.

The United States Brewers Association founded in 1862 is the oldest trade association in continuous operation in North America;[5] this indicates the importance of beer as an economic commodity in the early history of this country.

Fermented Products

Since prehistoric times, ethyl alcohol has been produced through a "natural" process known as *fermentation*. During fermentation, alcohol and carbon dioxide are produced when a mixture of *biological catalysts* called *enzymes* found in yeast cells act on the sugars found in fruits and berries. The enzymes in the yeast cells are known chemically as zymase. The chemical equation for the process is as follows:

$$C_6H_{12}O_6 \quad + \quad H_2O \xrightarrow{\text{Yeast}} 2C_2H_5OH \quad + \quad 2CO_2$$

(Simple Sugar)   (Ethyl Alcohol)   (Carbon Dioxide)

All that is really needed to produce alcohol then, is simple sugar from fruits and berries, yeast and mild warmth. The fermentation process, if left undisturbed, will continue until a chemical mixture (wine) is produced having approximately 14 percent alcohol. When the mixture reaches 14 percent alcohol, the fermentation process ceases because the alcohol content at this level kills the yeast cells.

Wines. Most wines are produced by fermentation of grapes, but other fruits and berries can be used. White wine results from using white grapes or red grapes with the skins removed. Red wines are produced by using red grapes and retaining the red skins. Rosé wines are made by removing the red skins shortly after fermentation begins.

If the process of fermentation is allowed to continue it will eventually convert all the sugar to alcohol and a "dry" wine results. Claret and Chianti are popular dry red wines. Sauterne, Moselle and Rhine wine are dry white wines. Dry wines form no "beads" in the glass and are known as "still" wines.

Wine can be bottled prior to completion of the fermentation process, thus retaining some of the carbon dioxide. The retained carbon dioxide causes a powerful popping noise when the cork is pulled. The dissolved carbon dioxide is seen in the form of tiny bubbles, thus the name sparkling burgundy and bubbling champagne. The alcohol content in champagne is approximately 12 percent.

If the fermentation process is stopped early, a "sweet" wine results. Also some wines are carbonated before bottling by the addition of small amounts of sugar.

Natural wines are low in alcohol content (12–14 percent), but man soon learned to raise the alcohol content by the addition of alcohol distillates. These wine beverages containing more than 14 percent alcohol by volume are known as *fortified wines.* Sherry, port, vermouth and muscatel are fortified wines.

Beer and Ales. Beers and ales are produced by using cereal grains, such as corn, barley, rye and wheat. Since cereal grains contain starch instead of sugar, the starch must be converted to sugar before fermentation can begin. This is accomplished by a process called *malting.* The resulting malt (maltose) is then mashed and mixed with water. Enzymes convert the starch to sugar. At this point hops and yeast are added and fermentation begins. The hops give the beer its characteristic bitter taste. Substances called "congeners" are also found in beer and sometimes in wines. Examples of congeners are dextrine, vitamins, organic acids, salts, carbon dioxide, etc. Beers have an alcohol content of 3–6 percent. In Japan, rice is the grain used to make beer. It is called *sake* and has an alcohol content of 12–16 percent. Ales are malted the same as beer and have a slightly higher alcohol content than regular beer.

Fermenting mash has a crater-like appearance, as shown in Figure 3-1.

In the alcohol industry, fermentation occurs in closed-type fermenters with controlled temperature and under sanitary condi-

FIG. 3-1 Photograph of Fermenting Mash *(Courtesy Distilled Spirits Council of the United States,* **Inc.***)*

tions. This is in sharp contrast to the equipment used in the moonshine industry, where poor sanitation prevails. Figure 3-2 shows a closed type fermenter.

Distilled Products

Man has been able to increase alcohol concentration (proof rating) through a process called *distillation.* Alcohol has a lower boiling point than water and when a solution containing alcohol (fermented product) is boiled, the alcohol boils off first and the vapors can be collected and cooled, forming a solution with a much higher alcohol concentration. Today the processes of fermentation and distillation are carefully controlled. Figure 3-3 shows an operating control room for grain spirits and whiskey distillation system.

Distillation, then, is used to produce the so-called "hard liquors," such as the whiskeys, vodkas, gins, brandies etc. Each of the liquors consists chiefly of a mixture of alcohol and water. Raw whiskey is colorless, clear and not very palatable. Most whiskies are artificially flavored with caramelized sugars. The product is stored in charred barrels where aging deepens the color and charcoal absorbs

FIG. 3-2 Photograph of Fermenting Tanks (*Courtesy Distilled Spirits Council of the United States, Inc.*)

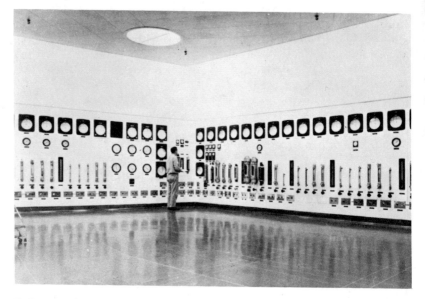

FIG. 3-3   Photograph of Operating Control Room *(Courtesy Distilled Spirits Council of the United States, Inc.)*

the bad tastes. The aging process is government supervised. "Bottled in Bond" means the aging process is not less than 4 years and the solution is 100 proof. Figure 3-4 shows the source and method of preparation of some alcoholic beverages.

ALCOHOL AND THE ECONOMY

Today the beverage alcohol industry represents a multibillion-dollar economic enterprise in the United States. It has become a well-established part of our national economy. In 1974 (a recession year) there were approximately 540,000 alcohol-related firms, mostly retail in nature, with 1.9 million employees whose wages totaled 10.8 billion dollars.[6] The jobs range from workers and owners in retail outlets such as liquor stores, supper clubs and small taverns to distillery workers, brewery workers and corporate executives. Somewhere in between are thousands of support workers doing bookkeeping, accounting, etc. Most visible to the public are the thousands of bar owners, bartenders, waitresses, liquor store clerks and truck drivers.

In addition, the alcohol beverage industry spends billions for

Type of Whiskey	Source	Process of Manufacture
Bourbon	Fermented Grain Mash. Not less than 51% corn.	Distillation
Rye	Fermented Rye Malt.	Distillation
Scotch	Fermented Barley Malt. Peat fires used in malting give smokey taste.	Distillation
Gin	Primarily from corn. Artificially flavored by filtering through Juniper Berries	Distillation
Vodka	Rye, Barley and sometimes potatoes. (Pure alcohol water)	Distillation
Brandy	Fermented grape wines.	Distillation
Rum	Molasses obtained from Sugar Cane	Distillation
Wines	Sugar from fruits and berries	Fermentation
Beer	Cereal grains	Fermentation

FIG. 3-4 Source and Method of Manufacture of Various Alcoholic Beverages

goods and services which directly benefit a wide cross-section of other industries and their employees. For example, the brewing industry alone consumes the grain output from more than 4 million acres of farmland.[7]

On the average the brewing industry also expends annually the following for goods and services:[8]

Fuel, Power and Water	$ 60,000,000
Transportation	295,000,000
Brewery Equipment and Improvements	160,000,000
Advertising and Promotion	240,000,000

The tremendous network of workers paying income taxes, plus the direct and indirect taxes on liquor itself and the corporate income taxes of the industry represent large sources of income for our local, state, and federal governments. In a recent year, the beverage alcohol industry generated 10.8 billion in revenues, 9.0 billion in public taxes and fees and 1.8 billion in corporate and personal taxes.[9]

The alcohol beverage industry must be considered a high-profit industry at all levels. Despite this, the brewing industry, through taxes, earns more for the government than it does for itself. For example, each barrel of beer or ale sold earns the government a total over $13 ($9 federal excise plus an averaged amount for all state excises). The brewing industries profit per barrel after taxes is estimated at a little over a dollar.[10]

Obviously, the sudden prohibition of alcoholic beverages would have great financial and employment repercussions. It is extremely doubtful that our society would ever attempt prohibition again, despite the fact that alcohol abuse and alcoholism present serious public health problems. However, if society were making a decision today on the legalization of alcoholic beverages, it is possible that it might, if it understood the evidence concerning alcohol abuse, refuse to sanction the sale of the beverage for human consumption. Since prohibition is ineffective and since the real problem is not alcohol itself but the people who use the drug, perhaps educational programs should be more realistic and emphasize the importance of responsible drinking as well as early recognition of developing alcoholism.

RATES OF ALCOHOL CONSUMPTION

A majority of American adults drink to some extent. Alcohol is a socially acceptable drug. In fact, the use of alcoholic beverages is considered normal behavior in most circles. It is used in social gatherings, to close business deals, as a food, as a medicine, as an intoxicant, as a thirst quencher and even in religious rituals. Whether a person drinks at all, how much he drinks and when he drinks usually depend on a variety of sociocultural factors.[11]

In this section, a series of tables and figures illustrate the extensive use of alcohol in this country. Since Prohibition the number of drinkers in this country has been on the increase. This has been accompanied by a corresponding decrease in the number of abstainers. The largest increase in the number of adult drinkers is among women.[12]

An alarming number of high-school-age and younger drinkers are surfacing, and we are seeing more alcohol-related problems among children in the 12–15 age range; there are even reported cases of alcoholism in children as young as 8 or 9.

Tables 3-1, 3-2 and 3-3 show the amount and type of alcoholic

Table 3-1. Per Capita Consumption of Malt Beverages (Gallons)

STATE	TOTAL POPULATION								21 YEARS AND OVER							
	1966	1967	1968	1969	1970	1971	1972	1973	1966	1967	1968	1969	1970	1971	1972	1973
Alabama	6.7	7.3	8.5	8.8	9.6	10.8	12.2	13.1	11.8	12.8	14.0	15.2	16.4	18.4	20.4	21.6
Alaska	12.9	15.2	15.4	16.7	17.8	20.2	18.6	19.6	25.9	31.6	32.0	34.1	32.9	37.3	35.1	36.7
Arizona	17.5	18.1	19.1	21.0	21.8	22.6	24.7	25.9	31.9	33.0	33.6	37.6	37.5	38.9	41.6	43.5
Arkansas	8.2	9.0	10.1	10.6	11.6	12.9	13.0	13.2	14.2	15.4	17.1	17.7	19.2	21.2	20.9	22.0
California	16.1	16.4	17.0	17.7	18.2	18.8	19.6	20.3	27.1	27.6	27.7	29.5	29.7	30.6	31.5	32.3
Colorado	15.6	16.3	17.0	18.1	19.1	19.9	21.4	22.7	27.1	28.3	29.5	30.9	32.4	33.7	35.6	37.5
Connecticut	16.1	16.2	16.2	16.3	15.0	16.4	16.0	17.3	26.5	26.7	26.4	26.6	26.6	26.5	25.6	27.4
Delaware	17.6	17.9	18.0	19.0	18.7	19.6	20.1	20.1	31.1	31.5	31.4	33.1	31.8	33.4	33.6	33.3
Dist. of Col.	23.5	22.8	22.7	22.8	23.6	24.1	23.0	23.7	37.9	37.4	36.2	37.7	36.8	37.0	35.5	36.5
Florida	15.2	16.3	16.7	17.7	18.4	20.4	22.0	23.3	24.9	26.8	26.9	28.7	28.8	31.7	33.7	35.6
Georgia	8.3	9.2	10.2	11.4	12.7	13.9	14.8	15.4	14.8	16.4	18.2	19.9	21.6	23.8	24.9	25.8
Hawaii	13.1	14.2	15.2	14.5	17.7	17.8	17.4	17.3	24.3	26.4	27.1	26.2	30.3	30.5	29.7	29.1
Idaho	15.0	15.7	16.2	17.4	19.1	20.3	21.8	22.6	26.8	27.9	28.6	30.1	33.2	35.3	37.3	38.4
Illinois	19.3	18.9	19.1	19.1	19.8	20.1	20.0	20.3	32.2	31.6	32.0	32.7	32.6	33.0	32.5	32.8
Indiana	15.3	15.4	15.7	16.0	16.2	16.3	16.4	16.8	26.3	26.5	27.0	27.1	27.4	27.5	27.3	27.6
Iowa	16.2	16.3	16.5	16.8	17.8	18.2	18.4	19.3	27.3	27.4	27.9	27.8	29.6	30.3	30.0	31.2
Kansas	11.0	11.2	12.1	12.7	14.2	14.9	15.8	16.6	18.5	18.8	20.4	20.9	23.2	24.4	25.4	26.5
Kentucky	12.9	13.5	13.8	14.3	15.3	15.9	16.4	16.7	22.4	23.4	24.0	24.1	25.6	26.7	27.0	27.4
Louisiana	15.4	16.1	16.4	17.3	18.8	18.7	19.6	20.2	28.3	29.6	30.1	31.2	33.6	33.3	34.2	34.9
Maine	16.6	17.5	18.3	19.3	20.1	21.1	21.7	22.8	28.4	29.9	30.8	32.3	33.5	35.2	35.8	37.1
Maryland	19.9	19.9	20.0	20.7	21.1	21.0	20.6	21.6	34.6	34.6	34.4	35.4	35.3	35.1	34.1	35.3
Massachusetts	17.5	17.8	18.3	18.9	18.9	19.1	19.6	21.3	28.7	29.2	29.8	30.6	30.7	31.0	31.3	33.6
Michigan	21.3	21.0	21.3	21.3	21.9	21.7	22.2	23.2	37.3	36.6	37.6	36.8	37.7	37.4	37.6	38.9
Minnesota	16.9	16.8	17.0	17.5	18.2	18.5	18.3	20.1	29.5	29.3	29.8	30.0	31.2	31.7	30.7	33.5
Mississippi	7.9	9.0	10.0	11.5	12.9	14.7	15.3	16.1	14.8	16.7	18.1	20.7	23.0	26.1	26.7	27.8
Missouri	17.7	16.9	17.4	18.1	18.6	18.8	19.0	19.5	29.1	27.8ʳ	28.7	29.4	30.2	30.5	30.4	31.1
Montana	20.8	21.8	21.7	22.3	24.1	25.4	25.0	27.7	36.9	38.6	37.3	38.7	42.4	43.5	42.0	46.1
Nebraska	18.0	18.9	19.6	20.4	21.0	22.2	21.1	22.7	30.5	32.1	32.8	34.1	34.9	36.8	34.4	36.7
Nevada	23.4	24.2	25.6	27.6	27.9	28.6	30.1	31.9	40.6	42.3	41.0	48.4	45.8	47.1	49.5	52.1
New Hampshire	22.4	23.1	23.9	25.6	27.2	29.1	29.7	31.9	37.5	38.7	39.6	42.1	45.3	48.5	48.3	51.6
New Jersey	18.8	18.6	18.9	19.0	19.3	19.2	18.7	19.5	30.7	30.4	30.4	30.6	31.0	30.8	29.7	30.8
New Mexico	14.6	15.2	16.3	17.7	18.4	20.0	21.8	21.6	28.9	30.0	30.9	34.2	33.7	36.7	39.2	38.4
New York	18.6	18.7	18.9	19.3	19.7	19.5	19.3	19.7	30.8	29.9	29.3	30.6	31.2	30.8	30.2	30.6
North Carolina	7.5	8.9	9.5	10.4	11.7	12.9	13.4	14.7	13.2	15.6	16.6	17.8	19.8	21.8	22.1	24.1
North Dakota	16.2	16.6	17.6	18.5	19.5	20.5	20.9	21.1	29.1	29.7	30.3	32.3	33.8	35.6	35.3	35.3
Ohio	18.1	18.6	18.7	18.4	19.7	19.5	19.4	20.0	30.9	31.7	31.8	30.9	33.0	32.6	31.9	33.2
Oklahoma	9.8	10.3	11.2	11.9	13.0	13.4	14.5	15.4	16.1	17.0	18.5	19.3	21.0	21.7	23.2	24.4
Oregon	16.8	17.4	17.6	18.7	19.5	20.1	20.9	20.8	27.9	28.8	28.7	30.2	31.8	32.8	33.4	32.9
Pennsylvania	20.5	20.1	20.5	20.7	21.1	21.3	21.4	22.0	33.3	32.5	33.3	33.0	33.7	34.2	33.8	34.4
Rhode Island	21.2	21.5	21.4	21.9	21.4	21.6	22.9	22.5	34.6	34.6	34.9	35.2	34.5	34.5	36.2	35.3
South Carolina	9.0	9.8	10.9	11.4	12.7	13.9	15.0	16.3	16.7	18.1	20.0	20.4	22.4	24.5	25.9	27.7
South Dakota	12.2	12.9	13.9	14.3	15.0	16.0	16.8	17.2	21.8	22.8	23.7	24.8	25.9	27.5	28.3	28.6
Tennessee	10.4	11.1	11.9	13.1	14.3	15.6	16.2	17.2	17.7	18.8	20.1	21.6	23.7	25.7	26.3	27.6
Texas	17.2	18.0	19.2	20.2	21.1	22.1	22.9	23.9	30.4	31.8	33.4	35.1	36.5	37.7	36.5	39.9
Utah	9.4	9.5	9.6	10.5	11.5	11.8	12.4	12.9	18.1	18.2	17.9	19.6	21.4	21.9	22.7	23.6
Vermont	19.8	20.5	21.2	21.7	22.3	24.2	24.9	24.0	33.9	34.9	36.8	36.0	38.0	41.2	41.8	39.8
Virginia	13.6	14.2	15.0	16.3	18.2	17.3	16.3	17.5	23.6	24.7	25.6	27.6	30.3	28.8	26.8	28.7
Washington	17.1	18.1	18.2	18.8	19.6	20.3	20.6	22.0	29.0	30.7	32.7	31.1	32.5	33.6	33.5	35.4
West Virginia	11.6	12.0	12.5	12.6	14.4	14.9	14.9	15.4	19.7	20.2	21.0	20.4	23.5	24.4	23.7	24.3
Wisconsin	27.0	26.8	27.2	28.2	27.5	28.2	28.5	29.3	46.7	46.3	46.8	47.9	46.9	48.0	47.5	48.3
Wyoming	15.7	16.7	17.8	19.2	20.7	21.5	23.0	25.5	27.7	29.5	30.3	33.1	35.2	36.6	38.6	42.3
Total	16.4	16.7	17.2	17.8	18.6	19.0	19.4	20.2	27.9	28.4	28.9	29.7	30.8	31.4	31.6	32.7

SOURCE: Brewers Almanac, United States Brewers Association, Inc., 1975

33

Table 3-2. Per Capita Consumption of Wine (Gallons)

STATE	TOTAL POPULATION								21 YEARS AND OVER							
	1966	1967	1968	1969	1970	1971	1972	1973	1966	1967	1968	1969	1970	1971	1972	197:
Alabama	.23	.25	.31	.34	.41	.43	.46	.49	.40	.44	.51	.57	.70	.74	.76	.8(
Alaska	.87	1.04	1.02	1.26	1.54	1.86	1.95	2.09	1.82	2.22	2.19	2.71	2.85	3.42	3.69	3.9:
Arizona	1.08	1.14	1.17	1.22	1.40	1.61	1.75	1.74	1.97	2.09	2.14	2.23	2.44	2.79	2.95	2.9.
Arkansas	.49	.53	.53	.49	.62	.65	.69	.68	.82	.88	.86	.79	1.02	1.03	1.12	1.0!
California	2.17	2.26	2.41	2.65	2.93	3.16	3.44	3.57	3.69	3.84	4.05	4.47	4.78	5.16	5.51	5.6!
Colorado	.93	.98	1.10	1.17	1.41	1.75	1.91	2.03	1.65	1.74	1.96	2.05	2.41	2.96	3.18	3.3
Connecticut	1.27	1.31	1.33	1.42	1.56	1.71	1.78	1.82	2.11	2.17	2.18	2.32	2.53	2.76	2.85	2.8
Delaware	.86	.89	.96	.96	.96	1.08	1.34	1.38	1.50	1.54	1.65	1.68	1.64	1.84	2.23	2.2
Dist. of Col.	3.23	3.45	3.33	3.84	3.95	4.34	4.74	4.87	5.12	5.58	5.26	6.06	6.12	6.91	7.32	7.5
Florida	1.02	1.06	1.13	1.26	1.39	1.59	1.78	1.88	1.72	1.79	1.94	2.14	2.19	2.47	2.74	2.8
Georgia	.46	.49	.52	.62	.63	.57	.80	.83	.80	.86	.90	1.07	1.07	.97	1.34	1.3
Hawaii	.65	.70	.77	.84	1.12	1.69	1.36	1.66	1.18	1.23	1.32	1.44	1.93	2.89	2.32	2.7
Idaho	.32	.33	.36	.39	.44	1.17	1.38	1.30	.56	.58	.62	.66	.76	2.05	2.36	2.2
Illinois	.89	.95	.98	1.11	1.24	1.46	1.59	1.64	1.50	1.59	1.62	1.83	2.05	2.39	2.59	2.6
Indiana	.40	.42	.42	.46	.54	.61	.63	.78	.69	.73	.72	.78	.91	1.03	1.05	1.2
Iowa	.20	.21	.22	.24	.28	.34	.41	.45	.33	.35	.36	.39	.46	.56	.67	.7
Kansas	.30	.34	.36	.38	.43	.48	.59	.55	.49	.55	.58	.61	.70	.78	.95	.8
Kentucky	.30	.31	.33	.35	.38	.46	.51	.51	.51	.53	.56	.59	.64	.78	.83	.8
Louisiana	1.14	1.08	1.16	1.16	1.26	1.47	1.53	1.05	2.06	1.94	2.05	2.02	2.25	2.63	2.67	1.8
Maine	.34	.36	.37	.39	.44	1.85	1.22	1.20	.59	.62	.63	.66	.74	3.10	2.00	1.9
Maryland	.90	.94	.94	1.08	1.14	1.30	1.51	1.58	1.59	1.67	1.63	1.89	1.92	2.18	2.50	2.5
Massachusetts	1.07	1.10	1.13	1.25	1.39	1.74	1.88	1.96	1.80	1.85	1.89	2.09	2.26	2.83	3.01	3.1
Michigan	.75	.84	.82	.94	1.07	1.25	1.36	1.42	1.32	1.46	1.42	1.62	1.85	2.18	2.31	2.3
Minnesota	.54	.57	.60	.64	.70	.92	1.00	1.01	.95	1.01	1.05	1.11	1.21	1.57	1.69	1.6
Mississippi	—	.22	.25	.32	.36	.45	.57	.53	—	.38	.43	.54	.64	.82	1.00	.9
Missouri	.68	.69	.73	.69	.90	.87	.99	.94	1.11	1.12	1.18	1.12	1.47	1.41	1.59	1.5
Montana	.43	.47	.51	.56	.60	.67	.82	.88	.77	.83	.90	.96	1.03	1.15	1.37	1.4
Nebraska	.45	.45	.50	.51	.61	.75	.80	.74	.78	.78	.86	.88	1.01	1.24	1.12	1.2
Nevada	1.92	2.14	2.19	2.52	3.01	3.30	3.76	4.02	3.43	3.87	3.97	4.06	4.99	5.46	6.18	6.5
New Hampshire	.72	.82	.89	1.06	1.43	1.82	1.94	2.03	1.21	1.38	1.49	1.75	2.39	3.02	3.15	3.2
New Jersey	1.40	1.41	1.49	1.58	1.76	1.96	2.14	2.13	2.25	2.29	2.39	2.54	2.83	3.15	3.40	3.3
New Mexico	1.22	1.30	1.36	1.39	1.57	1.69	1.71	1.63	2.41	2.57	2.63	2.73	2.88	3.13	3.07	2.8
New York	1.58	1.61	1.60	1.74	1.86	2.10	2.29	2.37	2.52	2.57	2.54	2.73	2.96	3.32	3.58	3.6
North Carolina	.52	.48	.50	.62	.72	.91	1.10	1.07	.89	.82	.73	1.03	1.23	1.54	1.82	1.7
North Dakota	.39	.41	.41	.46	.48	.56	.82	.75	.70	.72	.72	.98	.84	.98	1.28	1.2
Ohio	.66	71	.75	.79	.85	.98	1.02	1.04	1.12	1.30	1.21	1.30	1.43	1.64	1.69	1.7
Oklahoma	.53	.60	.59	.59	.68	.81	.78	.89	.87	.97	.96	.94	1.11	1.31	1.24	1.4
Oregon	1.21	1.28	1.40	1.55	1.83	2.13	2.44	2.57	2.00	2.10	2.28	2.55	2.99	3.44	3.90	4.0
Pennsylvania	.77	.78	.78	.84	.90	1.02	1.12	1.12	1.24	1.27	1.26	1.34	1.45	1.64	1.77	1.7
Rhode Island	1.25	1.41	1.42	1.46	1.78	2.15	2.22	2.22	2.04	2.34	2.33	2.40	2.86	3.43	3.51	3.4
South Carolina	—	—	—	—	.74	.87	1.08	1.08	—	—	.93	.98	1.31	1.53	1.86	1.8
South Dakota	.47	.50	.53	.58	.60	.72	.83	.82	.84	.89	.92	1.02	1.04	1.25	1.39	1.3
Tennessee	.32	.32	.33	.39	.30	.48	.58	.61	.53	.54	.54	.63	.49	.80	.94	.9
Texas	.62	.66	.64	.47	.78	.89	1.02	1.03	1.07	1.14	1.10	.80	1.34	1.49	1.68	1.7
Utah	.43	.43	.44	.47	.52	.65	.72	.77	.82	.81	.83	.88	.98	1.20	1.32	1.4
Vermont	1.20	1.29	1.41	1.47	1.74	2.17	2.26	2.35	2.06	2.22	2.39	2.43	2.98	3.67	3.79	3.!
Virginia	.76	.80	.82	.86	.94	1.07	1.10	1.34	1.31	1.38	1.40	1.44	1.57	1.79	1.81	2.!
Washington	1.09	1.15	1.27	1.76	1.80	2.03	2.22	2.24	1.84	1.93	2.12	2.86	2.99	3.35	3.62	3.6
West Virginia	.36	.37	.38	.38	.41	.48	.51	.49	.59	.60	.61	.60	.68	.79	.82	.7
Wisconsin	.69	.72	.77	.81	.98	1.13	1.34	1.32	1.22	1.28	1.35	1.43	1.67	1.93	2.23	2.1
Wyoming	.50	.53	.57	.61	.71	.84	.98	1.03	.90	.94	1.03	1.09	1.21	1.41	1.62	1.7
Total	.98	1.03	1.07	1.17	1.31	1.48	1.62	1.61	1.65	1.74	1.74	1.85	2.18	2.37	2.56	2.6

Source: Wine Institute and United States Department of Commerce.

SOURCE: Wine Institute and United States Department of Commerce

Table 3-3. Per Capita Consumption of Distilled Spirits (Gallons)

STATE	TOTAL POPULATION 1966	1967	1968	1969	1970	1971	1972	1973	21 YEARS AND OVER 1966	1967	1968	1969	1970	1971	1972	1973
Alabama	.80	.88	.98	.98	1.12	1.25	1.34	1.38	1.41	1.54	1.70	1.83	1.83	2.12	2.24	2.28
Alaska	2.63	2.83	2.91	2.91	3.13	3.37	3.37	3.32	5.31	5.88	6.05	6.50	6.90	6.21	6.38	6.23
Arizona	1.29	1.39	1.47	1.66	1.67	1.77	1.85	1.88	2.35	2.54	2.67	2.80	3.12	3.04	3.12	3.15
Arkansas	.78	.81	.82	.97	1.47	.93	1.01	1.07	1.35	1.39	1.41	1.50	1.54	1.54	1.63	1.72
California	2.05	2.10	2.19	2.26	2.26	2.31	2.34	2.38	3.45	3.55	3.64	3.77	3.78	3.75	3.76	3.79
Colorado	1.61	1.75	1.78	1.98	1.93	2.06	2.13	2.23	2.79	3.04	3.07	3.37	3.47	3.50	3.55	3.68
Connecticut	2.32	2.38	2.48	1.99	2.40	2.38	2.39	2.39	3.82	3.92	4.05	4.08	3.89	3.86	3.83	3.79
Delaware	2.48	2.59	2.68	2.18	2.89	2.96	2.70	2.73	4.34	4.56	4.62	4.97	4.95	5.04	4.53	4.54
Dist. of Col.	7.44	7.39	7.32	7.66	7.57	7.70	7.44	6.92	12.00	12.10	12.03	12.65	11.28	11.99	11.50	10.67
Florida	2.34	2.46	2.60	1.10	2.66	2.62	2.79	2.72	3.85	4.04	4.25	4.00	4.64	4.09	4.28	4.14
Georgia	1.18	1.29	1.38	2.47	1.64	1.75	1.92	1.76	2.11	2.30	2.45	2.64	2.78	3.00	3.25	2.95
Hawaii	1.60	1.77	1.83	1.90	1.80	1.52	1.83	n.a.	2.97	3.31	3.33	3.44	3.15	2.60	3.12	n.a.
Idaho	1.02	1.05	1.10	1.14	1.19	1.24	1.28	1.28	1.83	1.87	1.94	1.97	2.06	2.16	2.19	2.16
Illinois	2.01	2.05	2.14	1.66	2.18	2.27	2.31	2.35	3.35	3.43	3.55	3.68	3.54	3.74	3.75	3.79
Indiana	.98	1.02	1.06	1.13	1.19	1.15	1.24	1.24ᵉ	1.68	1.74	1.81	1.90	2.01	1.94	2.06	2.05
Iowa	.96	1.02	1.07	1.64	1.12	1.17	1.19	1.26	1.63	1.71	1.77	1.83	1.83	1.94	1.94	2.04
Kansas	.91	.96	1.04	2.00	1.07	1.15	1.18	1.21	1.54	1.60	1.73	1.70	1.69	1.88	1.89	1.92
Kentucky	1.12	1.24	1.29	1.01	1.38	1.36	1.41	1.42	1.94	2.13	2.20	2.26	2.27	2.29	2.31	2.32
Louisiana	1.42	1.35	1.37	1.40	1.45	1.43	1.45	1.40	2.61	2.48	2.50	2.53	2.49	2.56	2.52	2.42
Maine	1.56	1.57	1.57	1.63	1.68	1.65	1.71	1.77	2.67	2.68	2.68	2.72	2.79	2.74	2.80	2.88
Maryland	1.80	1.91	2.03	2.18	2.23	2.34	2.42	2.49	3.13	3.32	3.50	3.73	3.89	3.93	4.00	4.08
Massachusetts	1.98	2.10	2.19	2.34	2.24	2.27	2.35	2.46	3.25	3.44	3.55	3.78	3.67	3.69	3.76	3.89
Michigan	1.44	1.47	1.56	2.00	1.70	1.71	1.78	1.80	2.52	2.57	2.70	2.88	2.89	2.95	3.02	3.02
Minnesota	1.59	1.77	1.81	1.11	1.85	1.96	1.89	2.00	2.79	3.08	3.13	3.53	3.23	3.36	3.17	3.32
Mississippi	.35	.74	.87	1.21	1.11	1.20	1.27	1.31	.66	1.38	1.58	1.77	1.85	2.15	2.22	2.27
Missouri	1.42	1.48	1.58	1.64	1.65	1.57	1.61	1.51	2.33	2.43	2.58	2.67	2.64	2.54	2.58	2.41
Montana	1.36	1.42	1.50	1.58	1.65	1.71	1.80	1.88	2.43	2.51	2.64	2.75	2.80	2.93	3.02	3.12
Nebraska	1.30	1.47	1.50	1.60	1.67	1.69	1.77	1.73	2.22	2.50	2.54	2.68	2.81	2.80	2.89	2.79
Nevada	4.00	4.41	4.61	5.16	5.11	5.31	5.95	6.37	6.93	7.72	8.16	9.07	9.46	8.73	9.76	10.38
New Hampshire	3.34	3.55	3.67	4.02	4.57	5.02	5.37	5.40	5.58	5.94	6.08	6.60	7.69	8.36	8.74	8.73
New Jersey	2.13	2.15	2.26	2.32	2.27	2.25	2.32	2.27	3.47	3.51	3.65	3.74	3.61	3.62	3.68	3.58
New Mexico	1.05	1.17	1.27	1.40	1.51	1.48	1.62	1.57	2.08	2.31	2.51	2.70	2.87	2.72	2.91	2.79
New York	1.94	2.01	2.27	2.29	2.38	2.36	2.19	2.35	3.10	3.21	3.63	3.65	3.71	3.73	3.43	3.66
North Carolina	1.19	1.28	1.38	1.46	1.49	1.50	1.51	1.53	2.10	2.24	2.38	2.48	2.47	2.53	2.51	2.51
North Dakota	1.33	1.39	1.49	1.73	1.67	1.71	2.00	2.05	2.38	2.48	2.62	2.96	2.81	2.98	3.38	3.44
Ohio	1.35	1.34	1.31	1.34	1.32	1.31	1.33	1.37	2.31	2.28	2.23	2.26	2.17	2.20	2.20	2.25
Oklahoma	1.08	1.16	1.23	1.31	1.39	1.34	1.32	1.44	1.78	1.92	2.00	2.11	2.23	2.17	2.11	2.28
Oregon	1.36	1.38	1.47	1.54	1.50	1.52	1.58	1.66	2.25	2.27	2.39	2.49	2.47	2.47	2.53	2.62
Pennsylvania	1.22	1.27	1.32	1.34	1.37	1.39	1.41	1.44	1.99	2.05	2.12	2.13	2.15	2.23	2.22	2.25
Rhode Island	1.64	1.79	1.92	1.98	1.96	2.00	2.07	2.14	2.69	2.94	3.12	3.18	3.22	3.20	3.27	3.35
South Carolina	1.63	1.67	1.68	1.81	2.00	1.95	2.10	2.08	3.01	3.08	3.07	3.23	3.40	3.45	3.61	3.55
South Dakota	1.24	1.29	1.45	1.54	1.46	1.59	1.57	1.76	2.20	2.28	2.56	2.66	2.52	2.74	2.65	2.93
Tennessee	.88	.87	.89	1.10	.96	.99	1.10	1.19	1.50	1.48	1.48	1.67	1.53	1.64	1.78	1.91
Texas	1.01	1.07	1.12	1.19	1.22	1.26	1.26	1.30	1.78	1.89	1.97	2.06	2.11	2.14	2.12	2.17
Utah	.84	.84	.86	.87	.88	.90	.94	.96	1.61	1.61	1.64	1.63	1.64	1.66	1.72	1.75
Vermont	2.26	2.41	2.65	2.71	2.79	2.90	3.17	3.23	3.88	4.10	4.42	4.50	4.75	4.94	5.30	5.36
Virginia	1.47	1.53	1.60	1.66	1.66	1.68	1.71	1.76	2.55	2.67	2.74	2.82	2.79	2.80	2.82	2.88
Washington	1.61	1.68	1.71	1.73	1.77	1.76	1.74	1.83	2.73	2.84	2.86	2.87	2.98	2.91	2.83	2.96
West Virginia	.93	.97	1.02	1.04	1.14	1.26	1.29	1.33	1.58	1.67	1.68	1.69	1.76	2.05	2.07	2.10
Wisconsin	1.69	1.76	1.85	2.00	2.01	2.04	2.18	2.23	2.92	3.04	3.16	3.39	3.48	3.48	3.63	3.68
Wyoming	1.51	1.63	1.77	1.98	1.86	1.92	2.02	2.15	2.68	2.88	3.10	3.18	3.31	3.27	3.38	3.56
Total	1.58	1.64	1.73	1.80	1.83	1.85	1.89	1.92	2.68	2.79	2.91	3.01	3.05	3.07	3.08	3.10

a. Not available.
ource: Distilled Spirits Institute, Inc. and United States Department of Commerce.

SOURCE: Distilled Spirits Institute, Inc. and United States Department of Commerce

35

beverages consumed (not absolute alcohol) in the United States from 1966 to 1973. These figures are based on taxes paid and do not take into account home production or the moonshine industry.

Since these tables are for the years 1966–1973, they do not indicate the increase in drinking that has occurred since the days of Prohibition. In studying these tables one should use caution, especially in making state-by-state comparisons. For example, certain areas of the country attract a multitude of vacationers and tourists, e.g., Nevada and the District of Columbia. Also, there are price variations for alcoholic beverages from state to state, so that certain states tend to be low price centers. This causes an inflated picture of alcohol consumption in these areas, because people, especially automobile-borne transients, stock up on alcoholic beverages when they are in the low price areas.

To partially eliminate these effects, we have also included comparisons by larger geographic units. Figure 3-5 shows the ap-

APPARENT CONSUMPTION* OF ABSOLUTE ALCOHOL, IN U.S. GALLONS PER PERSON IN THE DRINKING-AGE POPULATION,** BY REGION, U.S.A. 1970

The Pacific and New England regions consume the greatest amount of alcohol, while the South Central regions consume the least.

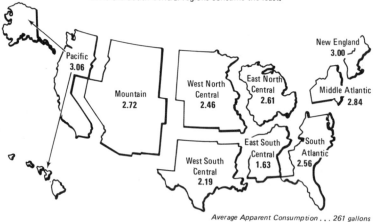

Average Apparent Consumption . . . 261 gallons

Note: The regions are the standard regions of the U.S. Census Bureau.
  For comparative purposes only. Amounts calculated according to tax–paid withdrawals.
  * Age 15+

FIG. 3-5   Consumption of Absolute Alcohol in the United States by Regions (Source: *Alcohol and Health,* First Special Report to Congress, U. S. Department of Health, Education and Welfare, National Institute on Alcohol Abuse and Alcoholism.)

parent consumption of *absolute alcohol* in U.S. gallons per person in the drinking age population, by region, for the year 1970. Remember, the absolute alcohol contained in the various alcoholic beverages varies with the proof rating. For example, a gallon of distilled spirits with a proof rating of 90 is approximately 45 percent absolute alcohol by volume. A gallon of wine with a proof rating of 24

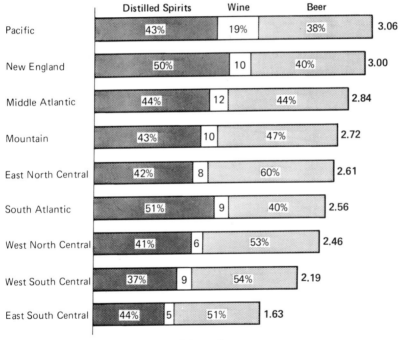

APPARENT CONSUMPTION* OF ABSOLUTE ALCOHOL
FROM ALL ALCOHOLIC BEVERAGES, IN U.S. GALLONS PER PERSON,
IN THE DRINKING-AGE POPULATION,** AND PERCENT OF
EACH MAJOR BEVERAGE CLASS, U.S.A. 1970

Inhabitants of the West South Central region consume only 37% of absolute alcohol from spirits and 54% from beer, while South Atlantic States consume 51% from spirits and 40% from beer. The Pacific region stands out by taking 19% of its alcohol in the form of wine.

Region	Distilled Spirits	Wine	Beer	Total
Pacific	43%	19%	38%	3.06
New England	50%	10	40%	3.00
Middle Atlantic	44%	12	44%	2.84
Mountain	43%	10	47%	2.72
East North Central	42%	8	60%	2.61
South Atlantic	51%	9	40%	2.56
West North Central	41%	6	53%	2.46
West South Central	37%	9	54%	2.19
East South Central	44%	5	51%	1.63

The regions are the standard regions of the U.S. Census Bureau.

*For comparative purposes only. Amounts calculated according to tax-paid withdrawals.
**Age 15+

FIG. 3-6 Consumption of Absolute Alcohol—From Different Alcoholic Beverages by Region—and Beverage Class (Source: *Alcohol and Health,* First Special Report to Congress, U. S. Department of Health, Education and Welfare, National Institute on Alcohol Abuse and Alcoholism.)

is only 12 percent absolute alcohol by volume. Figure 3-6 shows the apparent consumption of *absolute alcohol* from all alcoholic beverages, in U.S. gallons per person, in the drinking age population, and the percent of each major beverage class, i.e., distilled spirits, wine and beer.

In relation to Table 3-1, showing the consumption of beer, it should be pointed out that past industry surveys indicate 41 percent of all beer consumption is by persons between the ages of 21 and 34; 28 percent by those between 35 and 44; 18 percent by those between 45 and 54; and 14 percent by those 55 and older.[13] It should also be noted that in 1951, 41.6 percent of the total population was under 25 years of age. By 1973, the ratio had increased to 44.9 percent or approximately one-half of the population. This increase began in the late 1950's. Thus beer consumption has soared since that time.[14]

One should not underestimate the effects of home production or of the moonshine industry. Thousands of people enjoy the production of alcohol in their homes, mostly in the form of fermented products (beer and wine). Apparently the moonshine industry is on

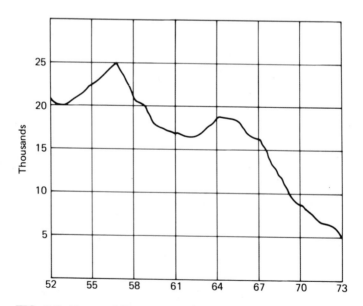

FIG. 3-7   Reported Detections and Seizures of Illegal Moonshine Operators 1952–73 (Adapted from Facts Book 1974.)

the decline, as indicated by Figure 3-7 which shows the number of illegal stills detected and seized during the years 1952–73.

Better surveillance and detection methods have played a role in the decline of this industry. In recent years, the increasing price of sugar has had an effect. The legalized alcohol industry can buy sugar in large bulk lots at cheaper prices than can the individual moonshiner. Also, the legal products use less sugar, because more time is allowed to complete the fermentation and distilling processes. The net result has been a trend toward equalization of prices, with the moonshiners suffering. There are reports that because of low profits many moonshiners are turning to the distribution of other drugs rather than run the high risk of illegal whiskey production at lesser profits. Figure 3-8 shows a photo of an illegal moonshine still in operation.

Despite these facts, there are apparently thousands of illegal moonshine operations still in existence, primarily in the southern states. American folklore has it that a few years ago a small town of about 50 people south of Roanoke, Virginia, had a higher sugar consumption than the entire city of Richmond, Virginia.

FIG. 3-8   Photograph of Illegal Moonshine Operation (Source: U. S. Treasury Department, Bureau, Alcohol, Tobacco and Firearms.)

PATTERNS OF ALCOHOL USE

Patterns of alcohol use range from nonuse to abuse, and include nondrinkers, light drinkers, moderate drinkers, problem drinkers and those physically and psychologically dependent on the drug alcohol.

Geography. There are many variables which affect the extent of alcohol use as well as the type of beverage used. For example, Figures 3-5 and 3-6 show geographical differences in alcohol consumption. The latest findings indicate that these geographical differences in drinking patterns are beginning to diminish. The more heavily urbanized areas contain the highest proportion of drinkers and heavy drinkers. These include the Middle Atlantic, New England, Pacific, and East North Central areas. The lowest proportion of drinkers is found in the East South Central states, other southern states and the mountain states.

In the southern states, large numbers of the population belong to conservative Protestant denominations whose tenets forbid drinking. This causes a high rate of abstinence in these areas.[15]

Education. Research indicates the highest proportions of abstainers are found among men and women with only grammar school education. Women college graduates were much more likely to be drinkers than other women but much less likely to be heavy drinkers if they do drink.[16] Women who had attended college but did not graduate had a higher proportion of drinkers than those who had graduated.[17]

The majority of college graduates, both men and women, were light or moderate drinkers. Men who graduated from high school and men who attended but did not complete college were most likely to be heavy drinkers.[18]

Occupation. There are rather wide variations in drinking patterns among occupational groups. Figure 3-9 shows some of these variations; of men who drink, those in the semiprofessional occupations show the highest proportion of heavy drinkers. The highest proportion of heavy drinkers among women who drink is among service workers.

PERCENT OF DRINKERS AMONG ADULTS* AND HEAVY DRINKERS AMONG ALL DRINKERS, BY OCCUPATION** AND SEX U.S.A. 1964-1965

Farm owners had the lowest percent of drinkers (60% of men and 26% of women) and also the lowest percent of heavy drinkers (20% of men and practically no women) among those who drank.

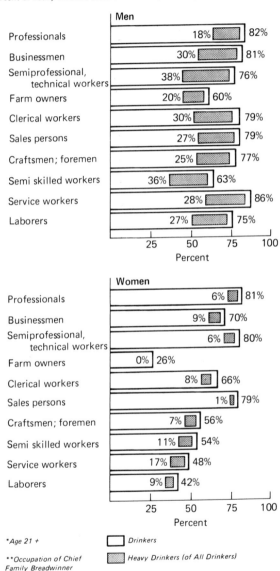

FIG. 3-9 Drinking Patterns of Various Occupational Groups (Source: *Alcohol and Health,* First Special Report to Congress, U. S. Department of Health, Education and Welfare, National Institute on Alcohol Abuse and Alcoholism.)

41

Other variables. There are many variables which affect drinking practices and patterns. These include such things as religious and ethnic backgrounds, parental attitudes and socioeconomic class. Space limitations prevent an adequate discussion of these, but the interested reader should refer to the *First Special Report to Congress on Alcohol and Health* listed in the bibliography of this chapter. It gives a comprehensive analysis of some òf the most recent surveys of American drinking practices.

METABOLISM OF ALCOHOL

Alcohol is ingested through the mouth and passes down the esophagus into the stomach. Since alcohol requires no digestion, a small amount is absorbed directly into the blood stream from the stomach. However, the major portion passes through the pyloric sphincter into the intestines. Most of the alcohol is then absorbed directly into the blood stream from the small intestines.

The circulating blood carries the alcohol to the various parts of the body. The liver is the organ most significantly involved in the processing of alcohol, and consequently, as we will learn later, is the organ most severely affected by the long abuse of alcohol. Alcohol is acted upon in the liver by the enzyme ADH (alcohol dehydrogenase) and the coenzyme NAD (nicotinamide adenine dinucleotide). The action of these enzymes on alcohol yields acetaldehyde which is oxidized to acetic acid. Acetic acid in turn yields energy, carbon dioxide and water. Figure 3-10 illustrates the metabolism of alcohol in the body.

The metabolism of alcohol in the body is evidenced by the fact that only a small amount of a given dose is excreted by the different routes available.[19] A small part (about 10 percent) of the absorbed alcohol is eliminated in an unmetabolized form through the kidneys, lungs and sweat glands.[20] The process of metabolizing excessive amounts of alcohol over long periods of time has several debilitating effects on the liver. These are discussed later in the section on alcohol-related disorders.

Alcohol is metabolized in the body at a fairly constant rate, although the oxidation rate varies from person to person and there is evidence that heavy drinkers may metabolize alcohol at a somewhat

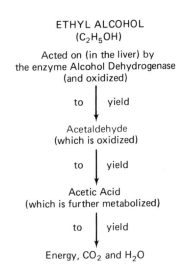

ETHYL ALCOHOL
(C_2H_5OH)

Acted on (in the liver) by
the enzyme Alcohol Dehydrogenase
(and oxidized)

to ↓ yield

Acetaldehyde
(which is oxidized)

to ↓ yield

Acetic Acid
(which is further metabolized)

to ↓ yield

Energy, CO_2 and H_2O

FIG. 3-10 Steps of Alcohol Metabolism
in the Liver

faster rate than others. The rate of oxidation in the average 150 pound man is approximately one-third of an ounce (absolute alcohol) per hour or two-thirds to three-quarters of an ounce of whiskey per hour.

As seen in Figure 3-10, when alcohol is metabolized in the body it gives off carbon dioxide, energy and water. Alcohol yields slightly over 7 calories per gram, which is roughly equivalent to 1 calorie per proof per ounce. In other words, 1 ounce of 100 proof distilled spirits yields approximately 100 calories. Beer and wines contain some unfermented sugars, other carbohydrates and additives, and thus have a slightly higher caloric content per proof per ounce. For example, a bottle of beer is roughly equivalent in absolute alcohol volume to 1 ounce of distilled spirits, but the bottle of beer contains approximately 135 calories.

Since the calories from alcohol yield nothing more useful than energy and contain no vitamins, minerals and proteins, beverage alcohol is not considered a true food. It cannot be stored in the body cells. However, other foods can be converted to fats and glycogens for storage in the body cells. Thus, a person who drinks and eats a normal diet is subject to weight gains, since the body will use the alcohol calories for energy first and convert the excess foods to fats and glycogen for storage.

To maintain body weight requires approximately 15 calories per pound per day. Anything more will result in a weight gain, while anything less will result in a weight loss. According to this formula a 200 pound man would require 3000 calories per day to maintain body weight. Suppose, for example, that a 200 pound man is receiving his required 3000 calories per day through food, but also has a cocktail every evening before dinner. If the cocktail contains 2 ounces of distilled spirits (100 proof), this represents 200 calories. If he mixes this with some carbonated beverage (probably another 65 calories), he is taking in an excess of 265 calories per day over his body requirements. Over a period of time a weight gain will ensue. It is easy to understand then why people who drink excessively and eat well gain weight; this is the source of the so-called "beer belly."

Conversely, if a person fails to eat the proper foods necessary to supply nutritional and body weight demands, and at the same time makes up the needed caloric intake through alcohol, he will begin to suffer from nutritional deficiencies.

BLOOD ALCOHOL CONCENTRATION

If a person drinks at a rate faster than the body can metabolize alcohol, the drug accumulates in the blood, having its first noticeable effect on the central nervous system. This occurs because alcohol cannot be stored in body tissues while awaiting metabolism nor can it readily be thrown off in significant amounts through other avenues such as the lungs, kidneys and sweat glands. The resultant accumulation is commonly referred to as blood alcohol concentration (BAC). Blood alcohol concentrations are expressed in terms of percentages: for example, a BAC of 0.05 percent would be 50 milligrams of alcohol per 100 milliliters of blood, and a reading of 0.10 percent would indicate 100 milligrams of alcohol per 100 milliliters of blood. A reading of 0.50 percent (a very high reading) would occur in a 150 pound man if he drank approximately one-fifth of 100 proof liquor within one hour. However, this same blood level could also result if the drinking were at a slower rate over a longer period of time.

Blood alcohol concentration can be determined by several methods, not only by testing blood samples. For example, the same information can be obtained by testing the breath, urine, saliva or even spinal fluid. If amounts of alcohol are found in these areas, then the corresponding amount of blood alcohol can be calculated.

Effects on motor skills and other body functions are fairly well established for the various blood alcohol concentrations, but there is considerable variability in the responses shown by different people at the various blood alcohol levels. There are also behavioral variations in the same people at different times. The following shows some *general* relationships between blood alcohol concentrations and behavioral responses.

0.02%	Pleasant feeling. Sense of warmth and well being. Minor impairment of judgment and memory.
0.03%	Doesn't worry. Time passes quickly. Feels superior.
0.04%	Motor skills may be impaired. Slight trembling of hands. Lots of energy.
0.05%	Lowered alertness. Increase in reaction time. Inhibitions almost gone. May become a lover or a fighter.
0.07%	Energy abated. Heavy pulse and slow breathing. Balance disturbed. Visual and hearing acuity reduced.
0.10%	Coordination badly affected. Less cautious. Staggers. Judgment and memory affected. May sing loudly.
0.20%	Has trouble standing up. Needs help to walk. Gross distortion of motor and sensory capability.
0.40%	Unconscious. Alcohol has become deep anesthetic.
0.60%	Near death. Depressed circulatory and respiratory functions. This may occur at 0.50 percent or lower in some individuals.

There are several blood alcohol charts available, usually in the form of handouts. These charts attempt to estimate blood alcohol levels that will occur in people by body weight after a given number of drinks. The charts however useful do not take into account the many variables affecting intoxication. We feel that they may be potentially dangerous, especially in the hands of people who do not fully understand that they are estimates only and may or may not apply to a given drinking situation. For that reason we are not including a sample blood alcohol chart here.

Intoxication

Intoxication occurs when a person builds up sufficient blood alcohol levels to cause body malfunctioning. This is the direct result of alcohol acting as a depressant on the central nervous system. The symptoms such as staggering gait, slurred speech, etc., are easily recognizable. However, some heavy drinkers are better able to conceal the effects of alcohol than are most moderate or light drinkers. Several factors do directly affect intoxication and are worthy of mention here. They are:

1. Amount of Consumption
2. Rate of Absorption
3. Rate of Oxidation
4. Tolerance
   a. Native
   b. Acquired

Amount of Consumption. When alcohol is ingested it must either be oxidized or eliminated unchanged through other avenues such as the lungs, kidneys and sweat glands. Only a small amount is eliminated unchanged. The rate of oxidation is approximately one-third to one-half ounce of alcohol per hour in a 150 pound man. A man ingesting alcohol at a rate faster than this could accumulate a high level of alcohol concentration in the blood. The total amount consumed over a period of time will have a direct effect on the alcohol blood level as well as the behavioral response.

For example if a person (150 pound man) were to consume 1 ounce of 80 proof whiskey per hour (approximately one-third to one-half ounce of absolute alcohol), in theory he should show no visible effects since the body is ridding itself of the alcohol at a corresponding rate. However if this person were drinking 3 ounces of the same spirits (three times the former rate) you can see that a buildup of alcohol must occur in the blood, since alcohol cannot be effectively stored in the body cells, but is continuously circulated throughout the body until it is oxidized or eliminated unchanged.

Alcohol is distributed evenly in the body fluids and cells, with the eventual concentration being proportionate to the water content in the organs and tissues. From the standpoint of intoxication then, it is unfortunate that the brain contains so much water and blood.[21]

The relationship between alcohol intake and degree of intoxication, while recognized by most people, is usually underestimated. The effects lead to high accident rates, arguments, fights, and other types of unusual behavior while intoxicated.

Rate of Absorption. Alcohol is absorbed into the bloodstream in about 30 to 90 minutes after ingestion. Remember that alcohol requires no digestion. Rate of absorption is affected by the amount of food in the stomach as well as by the type of alcohol being ingested.

Undigested food in the stomach delays the alcohol in reaching the small intestine where absorption into the bloodstream is more effective. Eating while drinking slows the rate of absorption and helps prevent peak blood concentrations. Spirits are absorbed faster than wine, which is absorbed more rapidly than beer.[22] Carbonated substances added to alcoholic beverages speed the rate of absorption because carbon dioxide relaxes the pylorus and allows alcohol to pass more readily into the small intestine. Sparkling burgundy and champagne have high carbon dioxide content because they are bottled before the fermentation process is complete, and are absorbed faster than some other alcoholic beverages.

Rate of Oxidation. The rate of oxidation is at a fairly constant rate of approximately one-third to one-half ounce per hour. There is some evidence that heavy drinkers may oxidize alcohol at a slightly higher rate than other people, but this has not been widely accepted by alcohol specialists. Often people will encourage an intoxicated person to walk or exercise in an effort to speed up the oxidation of alcohol. These activities have no appreciable effect in reducing BAC's. People often administer coffee to an intoxicated person to diminish the effects of alcohol. All that happens is that you have a wide-awake drunk on your hands. In other words the effects of intoxication will disappear only after the body has reduced blood alcohol concentration through its own natural processes of oxidation and excretion through the kidneys, lungs, etc.

Tolerance. Some people do build a tolerance to the effects of alcohol. Experienced drinkers therefore often are able to consume more alcohol with less effect than novice drinkers. (Later-stage alcoholics sometimes suffer a "reverse" tolerance, and then it takes less to get them intoxicated.) In addition, some people seem to have a native tolerance to alcohol, which diminishes its intoxicating effects. Body weight also acts as a tolerance factor. Since alcohol is distributed throughout the body it is diluted by body fluids. Heavier people have more body fluids and thus tend to have lower blood alcohol concentrations.

These variables help to explain why people exhibit different levels of intoxication with equal alcohol intake. No doubt psychological mood of the individual varies from one drinking experience to another and also has an impact on the intoxicating effects and behavioral responses to alcohol intake. This helps to explain why on a given night you seem to be able to drink more with fewer adverse effects than on other occasions.

EFFECTS ON THE CENTRAL NERVOUS SYSTEM

Alcohol is a depressant drug having a predominant and primary anesthetic effect on the central nervous system. The exact pharmacological mechanisms of this action are not completely understood; however, the ultimate effect is related to dosage. It may be that alcohol reduces the ability of the neurons to transmit impulses back and forth between the brain and the rest of the body.

The two most popular theories regarding the exact site in the brain where alcohol has its initial effect concern the *cerebral cortex* (higher brain centers, including the medulla) and the *reticular activating center* (RAS). The higher nerve centers control speech, memory, reasoning, behavior and other related functions. The reticular activating system (RAS) is located at the core of the brain and has a regulatory or integrating function. This coordinating unit must function properly to ensure the transmittal of impulses throughout the brain and is probably the initial site of alcohol impairment.

Apparently the RAS is affected at low blood alcohol levels, causing other areas of the brain to malfunction. The more complex behaviors such as judgment, learning and reasoning are affected first. This may manifest itself in major behavioral changes which are readily noticeable. Usually perception of oneself changes and the ability of self-criticism is diminished.

As the concentration of blood alcohol increases, motor coordination falters, movement becomes unsteady and reflexes are slower. Next the functions of the midbrain seem to be affected. This results in slurred speech, and poor control of the eye movements. Blurred vision is a result and the person appears glassy eyed.

When one reaches this stage and continues drinking, the blood alcohol level becomes dangerous. Alcohol begins affecting the lower nerve centers which control circulation and respiration. A coma (passing out) is likely to occur. At this point the person may be near death. One reason for not using alcohol as an anesthetic for surgery is that the dosage necessary to produce unconsciousness is close to the dosage which can produce death. Alcohol also slows blood clotting time.[23]

toward sex activity. It may create desire in some, but it does nothing to improve performance. As we mentioned earlier, it is impossible to predict the behavior of people under the influence of alcohol. Therefore it makes sense to consider the psychological make-up of the individual when we think of the effect of alcohol on emotions. Daily psychological mood swings may cause the same individual to react differently at different times under influence of the drug.

ALCOHOLISM AND ALCOHOL ABUSE

There are as many definitions of alcohol abuse and alcoholism as there are disciplines dealing with the problem. Some of these definitions are very general in nature and some very restrictive. For our purposes *alcoholism* is defined as *the excessive use of the drug to the point that it causes health, social or occupational problems.*

This definition does not concern itself so much with the amount of alcohol consumed as it does with the effect of the drinking problem on the key institutions in a person's life. The definition does indicate chronicity; in other words, a person must drink consistently enough over a period of time to cause severe problems.

These problems may manifest themselves in the form of a health problem, marital difficulties or trouble with friends. In terms of occupational problems, it could mean excessive absences, trouble with the boss or coworkers, a drop in productivity or even a job loss due to drinking. Alcoholics on the average annually miss 22 days more from work than nonalcoholics.

A central theme in most definitions is that alcoholism means loss of control over drinking. *Loss of control* refers to both the rate and amount of consumption, and is one way of detecting alcoholism. Once an alcoholic starts drinking, he cannot stop short of inebriation or, more precisely, he cannot stop drinking until the inner state of contentment is reached.

Not all alcoholics are physically dependent on (addicted to) alcohol. The test for physical dependence is the presence of withdrawal symptoms—i.e., anxiety, tremors, weakness, sweating, vomiting and diarrhea. Delirium tremens (DT's) are sometimes but not always present after the first stage of withdrawal and are characterized by hallucinations, disorientation and convulsions.[36] This is the most serious form of withdrawal illness. The physically addicted individual must drink to ward off the withdrawal symptoms.

Anyone who drinks to the point of inebriation is abusing the drug alcohol. Even the "social drinker" who occasionally drinks to the point of intoxication is abusing the drug, since he is exposing himself to loss of self control, accidents and other results of the disintegration of reasoning, motor control, etc. Alcoholism is the severest form of alcohol abuse.

There are also millions of so-called problem drinkers or hard drinkers in this country. These people drink to the point of intoxication quite frequently and often manifest some of the same symptoms as the physically addicted, except that they can stop drinking prior to intoxication and they can stop entirely if they choose. Some people drink heavily for years and then suddenly stop or cut down considerably on their drinking. One would think that these hard drinkers or problem drinkers would eventually become physically addicted to the drug. Apparently there is a fine line between being physically addicted and not being physically addicted. Herein lies one of the mysteries of alcoholism and alcohol abuse.

Types of Alcoholism

There is such great variation in individual drinking behavior that many authorities believe there is more than one type of alcoholic. Terms such as *periodic alcoholic, week-end alcoholic* and *frequent alcoholic* are often used. E. M. Jellinek made the following classification of types of alcoholism:[37]

1. *Alpha Alcoholism:* a psychological dependence on alcohol to relieve mental and physical pain. Although the drinking is undisciplined by most standards such as time, locale, amount and effect of drinking, it does not lead to loss of control.
2. *Beta Alcoholism:* heavy drinking has occurred long enough to manifest such alcoholic disorders as polyneuropathy (nerve damage), gastrointestinal disturbances and cirrhosis of the liver, etc. The heavy drinking in this case is motivated by customs of a social group. No psychological or physical dependence develops.
3. *Gamma Alcoholism:* characterized by increased tissue tolerance, withdrawal symptoms (physical dependence), and loss of control. Both physiological and psychological dependence are involved. Great damage psychologically, physically and socially occur with

Gamma alcoholism. The individual has the ability to abstain but loses control once the drinking starts. He can go on the wagon. This is the major type of alcoholism in America, Canada and the Anglo-Saxon countries.

4. **Delta Alcoholism:** similar to Gamma alcoholism except that in addition to loss of control there is also inability to abstain.

Alcoholism as a Disease

The problems of alcoholism and alcohol abuse are not new. They have gradually descended upon an ill-prepared society since the beginning of mankind. The abuse of alcohol has long been recognized as is evidenced by the fact that many societies have attempted control over the use of the beverage. Historically, efforts at control have met with ambivalence. In the final analysis these efforts have failed, an example being the Volstead Act of 1918. This act became the 18th Amendment to the Constitution in 1919, when Nebraska became the 36th state to ratify it. This amendment was then repealed by the 21st Amendment in 1933. This was the beginning of the end for most major efforts aimed at prohibition in the United States.

Despite all this concern over the problem, the concept of "alcoholism as a disease" was slow in evolving. This is partially because alcoholism is surrounded by an array of misconceptions. Even today many people consider the "skid-row derelict" to be the only true alcoholic. At the same time they consider the alcoholic immoral, weak in character, obstinate and a person to be shunned. The skid-row derelict represents visible evidence of the problem, but these unfortunate people represent only 3–5 percent of the total alcoholic population of this country. When people think of "skid row" or "the bowery" they think of an isolated section in a major city where alcoholics are concentrated, but every city and town has a skid row. It is only in the large cities that the concentration of alcoholics is heavy enough to attract major attention.

Alcoholics and alcohol abusers are found in business, in education, in industry and in every walk of life including the ministry. They are found at all educational levels and in all economic levels. They are found in the ghettos and slums of the inner cities and in the most affluent communities in the world. It is not an isolated problem.

Another problem inhibiting acceptance of the disease concept of alcoholism was the inability of authorities to agree on what actually constituted a disease. Disease is defined here as "a disturbance of function or structure of any organ or part of the body." Without question alcoholism manifests itself in a disturbance of body function and it has clearly recognizable symptoms.

Only in recent years has society started to change its attitude and accept alcoholism as a disease. One of the first major steps came in 1960 when E. M. Jellinek published a book entitled "The Disease Concept of Alcoholism." Much of this book was devoted to definitions and to describing alcoholism.

In June 1960, Joel Fort, M.D., an eminent authority in the field, was quoted in the San Francisco Chronicle as calling alcoholism the greatest public health issue in the nation.[38] Seven years later the District of Columbia passed the *Alcoholic Rehabilitation Act* which recognized alcoholism as more of a medical problem than a criminal issue. This statute said:

> All public officials in the District of Columbia shall take cognizance of the fact that public intoxication shall be handled as a public health problem rather than a criminal offense, and that a chronic alcoholic is a sick person who needs, is entitled to, and shall be provided adequate medical, psychiatric, institutional, advisory, and rehabilitative treatment services of highest caliber for his illness.[39]

This statute had many forward-looking features. It repealed the public intoxication statute, replacing it with a new provision prohibiting disorderly intoxication. It also established a comprehensive new system under civil law for detoxification, and inpatient and outpatient treatment for intoxicated persons and alcoholics. Under this statute, if a person is found intoxicated on the streets he may be taken home, but if this is not done he must be taken for detoxification and emergency medical treatment to the new detoxification center.

Since that historic act was passed many states have passed similar legislation, and many courts across the country have handed down rulings stating that if a person can be proven addicted, he cannot be held responsible for acts committed which are alcohol-related. The courts are frankly admitting that these acts are beyond a person's control, that he is suffering from a disease which renders him helpless to control his actions.

Alcoholism is now recognized as a disease by the World Health

Organization, The American Medical Association, The United States Public Health Service and many other authoritative groups around the world. In this country alone there are some 9 million alcoholics and alcohol abusers. As mentioned in Chapter 2, these statistics are probably on the low side since we rely heavily on police departments, hospitals and other agencies to gain these statistics. Obviously millions more probably never come into contact with such agencies. The estimated 9 million alcoholics and alcohol abusers represent 7 percent of the adult population. Any other disease affecting this many people would trigger the greatest rehabilitation and research program in history.

Cancer, heart disease and accidents are also major public health problems. Ironically, alcoholism also is related to these problems, and therefore fails to attract the attention it deserves.

Let us consider alcoholism and alcohol abuse in relation to some other major public health problems. In a recent year approximately 117,000 people needlessly lost their lives through accidents. Over 56,000 of these were in automobile accidents. Of the 56,000 over 50 percent were alcohol related. This represents over 28,000 alcohol-related deaths per year in traffic crashes alone, to say nothing of the number of disabling injuries that were the result of alcohol related crashes. We have no statistics indicating how many people died from other alcohol-related accidents such as falls in the house, but undoubtedly alcohol is a contributing factor in other accidents as well.

Through accidents and alcohol-related disorders the alcohol abuser shortens his life span from 10 to 12 years. Any phenomenon which is causing premature deaths at such an alarming rate must be considered a major public health problem. Aside from the human misery and the shortened lifespan, alcohol abuse is draining the economy of 15 billion dollars a year.

THE STAGES OF ALCOHOLISM

Alcoholism is apparently a progressive disease which passes through three identifiable stages, commonly called *early, middle* and *later* stages. Some people spend 5 to 15 years or longer progressing through all three stages; however, many alcoholics never reach the later stages, being killed accidentally or dying prematurely from some disorder which most often is alcohol related. The majority of alcoholics spend most of their alcoholic career in the early and middle stages. Since the disease is insidious and at times asymptomatic, especially in the early stages, the alcoholic and those around him fail to recognize what is happening. This has serious debilitating effects on a favorable prognosis.

Each stage of alcoholism is characterized by signs and symptoms which usually appear in clusters. Sometimes it is difficult to identify the exact stage a suspected alcoholic is in, since he often manifests the signs and symptoms of more than one stage at a time. Also, people progress through the various stages at different rates of speed. Some people, for unexplainable reasons, become alcoholics rapidly with very little drinking and others develop the disease slowly while drinking heavily. Others may drink heavily for years and never become alcoholic. No two people exhibit identical symptoms at the various stages.

Early Stages

It is important that one recognize all the signs of alcoholism, but recognition of the early signs is especially important. Like any other disease, alcoholism is more readily treatable in the early stages. If this were done the problem of alcoholism could be greatly reduced.

If used properly, alcohol does have very pleasant effects. It helps people to escape tension, anxiety, loneliness and other psychological problems. It is when people begin using alcoholic beverages exclusively and specifically for these purposes that they are taking their initial steps toward alcoholism. Escape-drinking is the beginning of a psychological dependence on a drug capable of producing addiction.

The symptoms characterizing the early stages include escape-drinking, guilt feelings, sneaking drinks, blackouts, and trouble stopping once the drinking starts. These are usually accompanied by an increased tolerance and it now takes more alcohol to achieve the same desired effects. Figure 3-13 shows some of the early signs of alcoholism.

Usually the individual spends more and more time thinking about drinking and often hurries to stop at a favorite bar even if it is out of his way. To see this particular phenomenon, you can go to a specified bar every day at the same time and observe the same

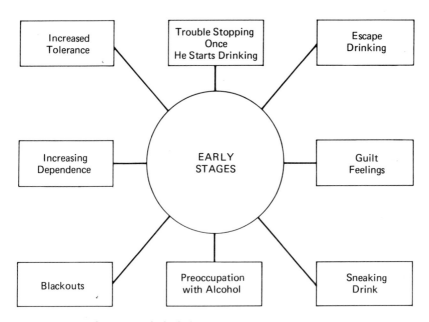

FIG. 3-13   Early Stages of Alcoholism

people coming into the bar at almost exactly the same time each day. In fact, after a while you can almost set your watch by their arrival. These people are showing a definite preoccupation with alcohol. This phenomenon occurs at most bars, even the well-appointed ones. It also occurs in many homes and offices. The problem of the housewife drinking alone at home is becoming increasingly common. Sneaking drinks and gulping drinks are other early danger signals. All of these indicate loss of control over drinking.

A definite early sign of developing alcoholism is the occurrence of *blackouts*. Scientists have yet to explain the physiological mechanism of blackouts. They should not be confused with passing out, however. *Passing out* is the result of the excessive intake of alcohol to the point where it has deep anesthetic effect, resulting in unconsciousness. In contrast, the *blackout* is loss of memory, a temporary type of amnesia. The blackout may be one in which the individual cannot remember even the major events occurring during an evening even though he appeared to be functioning well. Blackouts may also cover extended periods of time, even weeks if the intoxication is that prolonged.

We repeat, *blackouts are a definite sign of developing al-*

coholism; in fact the person may already be an alcoholic. Blackouts are easily detectable and should be regarded with deep concern.

Middle Stages

In the middle stages, the individual has lost control and the problem has become more severe. The hangovers become more severe and intolerable, and the guilt feelings become more intense, developing into self-hate. Figure 3-14 shows the symptoms characteristic of the middle stages of alcoholism.

It is here that the social and vocational problems usually become serious. The family of the alcoholic as well as his employers and friends become confused and disagreements often ensue. The alcoholic often uses these arguments as an excuse for more drinking. In effect, because of lack of understanding, friends, family members and work supervisors may be actually aiding the alcoholism at this point.

In an effort to regain control, the alcoholic will often change his drinking patterns. He will drink beer instead of martinis. He will set limits for himself and drink only one or two drinks in a given place, then go somewhere else to drink. He is losing control but in a

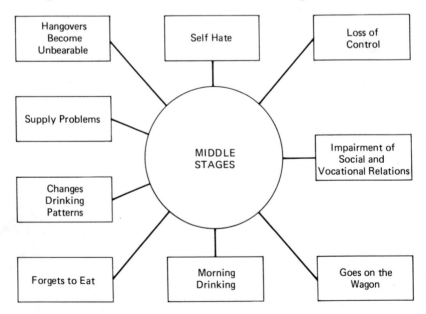

FIG. 3-14   Middle Stages of Alcoholism

different way. If he has an argument in a bar, he may avoid that particular bar entirely and go to another where he gains acceptance. Frequently it will be a lateral shift, to a bar with the same economic status as the previous bar. Inevitably new arguments will erupt or he will embarrass himself in the new surroundings. He may then shift to a lower class bar where again he finds acceptance. Of course, the end of this flight may be skid row; however, very few alcoholics make this complete transition. Also, most alcoholics, because of their financial status, avoid the unfortunate circumstances of a skid row. And many die prematurely due to alcoholic-related disorders or accidents before reaching the later stages of alcoholism.

Depending on financial status, supply becomes an acute problem. Even a wealthy alcoholic may hide his supply in an attempt to conceal the extent of his drinking. People moving into homes formerly occupied by alcoholics often find hidden bottles years later. The alcoholic becomes ingenious in protecting his supply. In effect alcohol has become his "God."

The middle stages are also characterized by attempts to go "on the wagon" (a slang expression for stopping drinking), but unless the alcoholic gets help he always goes back. He has lost control and has no power to regain it.

Finally, morning drinking starts as a way to ward off the unbearable hangovers and withdrawal symptoms. Morning drinking represents the final departure from "normal" drinking. Herein lies a common misconception. Many people feel that if you don't drink in the morning, you are not an alcoholic. Although many alcoholics never drink in the morning, morning drinking *is* a definite sign of alcoholism.

With morning drinking, the alcoholic closes a vicious circle —using alcohol to counter the effects of alcohol. He forgets to eat and the stage is set for the onset of nutritional deficiencies and many other alcohol-related disorders commonly found in the later stages of alcoholism.

Later Stages

At this stage, the disease has developed to the point that death may be close. Prolonged drinking episodes are common; the alcoholic lives to drink and is definitely using alcohol to control alcohol. He must drink to prevent the unbearable withdrawal symptoms. As mentioned earlier, the withdrawal symptoms are anxiety, tremors, weakness, sweating, vomiting and diarrhea. Delirium tremens (DT's) are sometimes present, characterized by hallucinations, disorientation and convulsions.

Medical attention during withdrawal is imperative, and even then the alcoholic may die. The withdrawal symptoms from alcohol are more severe than those from any other drug. We repeat, *medical attention is a must during withdrawal from alcohol.*

Many alcohol-related disorders are prevalent among those in the later stages of alcoholism. These are discussed in the next section. Figure 3-15 shows the characteristics of the later stages of alcoholism.

ALCOHOL-RELATED DISORDERS

Alcohol abuse and alcoholism are commonly associated with a large number of pathological conditions. The actual extent to which these conditions cause disability and even death is unknown. Also, the alcoholic seems to have more than his share of disorders which are not alcohol-related. They have exceptionally high rates of morbidity and mortality, and their lifespan is shortened by 10 to 12 years.[40]

A full discussion of the many alcohol-related disorders is beyond the scope of this book, but a few of the major ones are

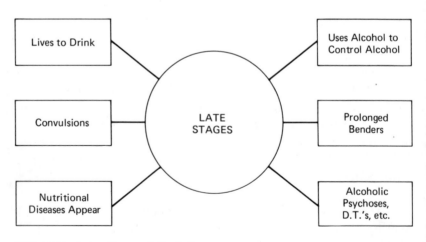

FIG. 3-15   Later Stages of Alcoholism

presented. Table 3-4 shows a partial listing of alcohol-related disorders found in man.

Most pathological conditions develop slowly over a long period of time after continuous consumption of excessive amounts of alcohol. Many of these conditions are actually the result of nutritional deficiencies rather than of alcohol itself; it is still unclear whether some are due to the alcohol directly or to a nutritional deficiency. Hopefully, research will eventually find the origin of all these disorders. It is a well-established fact that many heavy drinkers and alcoholics do not eat well-balanced diets. The failure to eat a well-balanced diet is often alcohol-connected, because many alcohol abusers substitute alcohol for food. As previously mentioned, alcohol does supply calories but they are used only for energy, leaving the alcohol abuser short of the many necessary proteins, amino acids, minerals and vitamins, especially folacin, niacin and thiamin. It should be pointed out that although nutritional deficiencies are readily observable on skid row, they are also common among the entire alcohol-abusing population, including those in excellent financial circumstances. First let us consider some neurological disturbances common among alcohol abusers.

Neurological Disorders

Wernicke's disease is an example of an alcohol-related disorder definitely known to be nutrition-related. Wernicke's syndrome presents a clinical picture of mental disturbance, ataxia of gait (uncoordinated), and paralysis of eye movement. Some cases show impairment of consciousness such as inattentiveness and slow and inadequate responses. The disease can be and often is fatal. It is associated with a severe deficiency of vitamin B_1 and responds well to treatment with thiamin.[41]

Korsakoff's psychosis is another nutritional deficiency disease and presents an interesting clinical picture. It is characterized by inability to recall recent events or form new memories. Confabulation is often present, i.e., the tendency to relate personal experiences of long ago as if they happened only yesterday. Fabrication is also common. The syndrome occurs with other conditions, but is very common in alcoholics. For example, traumatic Korsakoff's psychosis results from a stroke. Alcoholic Korsakoff's psychosis often

TABLE 3-4. Alcohol-Related Disorders

Gastrointestinal

Esophagitis
Esophageal carcinoma
Gastritis
Malabsorption
Chronic diarrhea
Pancreatitis
Fatty liver
Alcoholic hepatitis
Cirrhosis (may lead to cancer of liver)

Cardiac

Alcoholic cardiomyopathy
Beriberi

Skin

Rosacea
Telangiectasia
Rhinophyma
Cutaneous ulcers

Neurologic and psychiatric

Peripheral neuropathy
Convulsive disorders
Alcoholic hallucinosis
Delirium tremens
Wernicke's syndrome
Korsakoff's psychosis
Marchiafava's syndrome

Muscle

Alcoholic myopathy

Hematologic

Megaloblastic anemia

Vitamin deficiency disease

Beriberi
Pellagra
Scurvy

Metabolic

Alcoholic hypoglycemia
Alcoholic hyperlipemia

SOURCE: Alcohol and Health, First Special Report to Congress, U. S. Department of Health, Education and Welfare, National Institute of Alcohol and Alcoholism

follows delirium tremens and Wernicke's syndrome. The actual cause of alcoholic Korsakoff's psychosis is unknown but is probably a deficiency of a vitamin such as thiamin.

In contrast, neurological conditions such as delirium tremens and its variants, alcoholic epilepsy and alcoholic auditory hallucinosis, are not nutritional in origin.[42]

Gastrointestinal disorders

Alcohol has a multitude of injurious effects on the gastrointestinal system. The mouth, esophagus, stomach, intestines, pancreas and liver are all subject to harm from the alcohol abuse. The list of gastrointestinal disturbances in Table 3-4 is long and impressive. It is interesting to note that increased incidences of cancer appear in the mouth, stomach and esophagus. Cirrhosis of the liver also may lead to cancer.

Possibly the most widely known alcohol-related disorders in the gastrointestinal system occur in the liver. Alcohol has a toxic effect on the liver and is associated with such liver disorders as fatty liver, alcoholic hepatitis and alcoholic cirrhosis.

Data indicate that alcohol is hepatoxic in normal nonalcoholic people, independent of nutritional factors. Amounts of alcohol consumed by many "social" drinkers are sufficient to damage the liver, and one can sustain alcohol-induced hepatic injury without ever having been drunk.[43] Fat accumulation on the liver can occur rapidly; but the condition is reversible after consumption of alcohol stops.

Cirrhosis. Cirrhosis is a condition characterized by diffuse scarring of the liver. It is a very common complication of alcoholism. However, the pathogenesis is obscure. Recent research on a large homogeneous group of alcoholics indicates that the development of liver damage is dependent on the time and dose of alcohol abuse.[44]

Cirrhosis of the liver is a disabling and potentially fatal complication of alcoholism. The condition is irreversible, but the prognosis is much improved if the drinking stops. Those who have alcoholic cirrhosis and continue heavy drinking often die of hemorrhage from portal hypertension or of hepatic failure.[45]

For several years many authorities have recognized that the mortality rate from cirrhosis is related to alcohol consumption.

Terris evaluated mortality data for liver cirrhosis with respect to several parameters. He gave consideration to: long term trends; age, sex, and race; urban–rural differences; social class and occupation; and alcohol consumption. The evidence strongly supported the conclusion that cirrhosis mortality is directly related to consumption of alcohol from spirits and wine.[46]

Cardiac Disorders

The relationship between heart disease and chronic alcohol abuse has long been recognized, but the pathogenesis is unknown. The clinical picture often includes either slow or sudden onset of left- and right-sided congestive heart failure. Characteristic are a large heart, distended neck veins, narrow pulse pressure, elevated diastolic pressure and peripheral edema.[47] Absolute abstinence is necessary for successful treatment.

Other Alcohol-Related Disorders

A review of Table 3-4 will reveal a list of alcohol related disorders of the skin, muscle and blood. Alcohol affects most organs of the body.

TREATMENT OF ALCOHOLISM

Alcoholism can be treated and it can be arrested. Like other diseases, the earlier it is recognized, the better the prognosis. Unlike many other diseases, it cannot be cured through surgery, radiation therapy or drugs. Treatment for alcoholism entails arresting the disease, and then helping the person return to a normal, healthy and productive life. Since every alcoholic is different, the treatment must be individualized; it must be patient-centered to meet particular needs. The first requisite is an honest desire for help by the alcoholic himself. Without this all is lost, with it the prognosis is excellent.

Depending upon the individual, the desire for help usually comes after some crisis which causes the alcoholic to admit that he cannot control his drinking, and that he is powerless over alcohol. The more fortunate alcoholic may recognize this fact before alcohol has caused any real problems, while others go through a long series of crises, losing family, job and self-respect before admitting they have a problem with which they cannot cope. There are four components in the recovery process, shown in Figure 3-16.

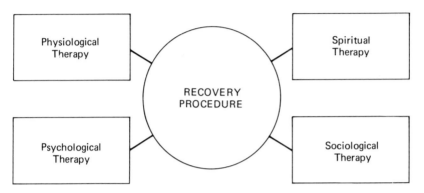

FIG. 3-16   Components of Alcoholism Treatment

These various components—psychological, physiological, sociological and spiritual—are closely interwoven. This indicates the need for close cooperation from several disciplines. The order in which these treatment components operate must be tailored to the individual. For example, the alcoholic may be sober at the time therapy begins, thus the withdrawal process is not necessary. Also the components may operate in combination with each other. We will briefly discuss each component. The order in which the components are applied in actual treatment situations varies from patient to patient and has no relation to the order in which they are presented in this discussion.

Physiological Therapy

Often, the alcoholic is physically addicted and must undergo a withdrawal process. This is different from medical treatment for acute intoxication and the two should not be confused. As mentioned earlier, the withdrawal symptoms from alcohol are anxiety, tremors, weakness, sweating, vomiting and diarrhea. Also delirium tremens (DT's) are often present and are characterized by hallucinations, disorientation and convulsions. Medical treatment is absolutely essential during the withdrawal process.

The medical procedures employed will depend on the severity of the situation. After detoxification is completed, tranquilizers such as reserpine and chlorpromazine are often utilized to reduce tension. The alcoholic is very susceptible to other diseases and to alcohol-related disorders, many of which are the result of nutritional deficiencies. Treatment of these conditions is individualized to meet the alcoholic's particular needs.

Sometimes aversion therapy is used. Aversion therapy is the employment of chemicals, hypnosis, etc., to create unpleasant associations with alcohol use. There are conflicting opinions about the value of this type of treatment, however.

Psychological Therapy

Psychotherapy takes many forms, including working with a trained counselor, group therapy and even self-analysis. The purpose is to gain self-respect and to change attitudes and feelings. The alcoholic must begin to understand himself, including both his strengths and weaknesses. He must understand how his behavior affects himself and others. Most of all he must want help to stop drinking.

Sociological Therapy

This may involve the alcoholic's friends, work supervisors and family, who must learn to cope and understand alcoholism. The alcoholic, to be successfully returned to society, must interact with the key institutions of his life. They, too, must interact with him and not be "enablers" or do things that cause him to revert to drinking. One example of this is constant nagging by family members—the alcoholic may use the nagging as an excuse for more drinking.

Spiritual Therapy

This involves faith—faith in God or faith in other things and other people besides himself. How the alcoholic does this is up to him, but in most cases it is an important aspect of his recovery.

Alcoholics Anonymous

Any discussion relating to recovery from alcoholism would not be complete without mention of Alcoholics Anonymous. This fellowship of men and women who share their common experience, strength and hope with each other has without question done more than any other individual or organization to promote recovery from alcoholism.

Alcoholics Anonymous had its beginnings in Akron in 1935 when a New Yorker on business there and successfully sober for the first time in years sought out another alcoholic. During his few months of sobriety the New Yorker noticed that his desire to drink lessened when he tried to help other "drunks" to get sober. In Akron he was directed to a local doctor with a drinking problem. Working together the businessman and the doctor found that their ability to stay sober seemed closely related to the amount of help and encouragement they were able to give other alcoholics.[48]

Numerically, A.A. consists of more than 1,000,000 men and women in the United States, Canada and about 92 other countries. These men and women meet in local groups which range in size from a handful of ex-drinkers in some localities to many hundreds in larger communities.

In the populous metropolitan areas, there may be scores of neighborhood groups, each holding its own regular meetings. Many A.A. meetings are open to the public; some groups also hold "closed meetings," at which members are encouraged to discuss problems which might not be fully appreciated by nonalcoholics.

The local group is the core of the A.A. Fellowship. Its open meetings welcome alcoholics and their families in an atmosphere of friendliness and helpfulness. There are now more than 28,000 groups throughout the world, including hundreds in hospitals, prisons and other institutions.[49]

The Twelve Steps of Alcoholics Anonymous are shown in Figure 3-17.

Today with an enlightened society that is finally beginning to accept alcoholism as a disease, we are on the threshold of making bigger breakthroughs in the prevention and treatment of alcoholism. The final solutions will come through research, education, treatment and rehabilitation. This will take a cooperative effort by many disciplines, and will need the full support of society.

THE TWELVE STEPS

1. We admitted we were powerless over alcohol—that our lives had become unmanageable.

2. Came to believe that a power greater than ourselves could restore us to sanity.

3. Made a decision to turn our will and our lives over to the care of God as we understood him.

4. Made a searching and fearless moral inventory of ourselves.

5. Admitted to God, to ourselves and to another human being in the exact nature of our wrongs.

6. Were entirely ready to have God remove all these defects of character.

7. Humbly asked Him to remove our shortcomings.

8. Made a list of all persons we had harmed and became willing to make amends to them all.

9. Made direct amends to such people wherever possible, except when to do so would injure them or others.

10. Continued to take personal inventory and when we were wrong promptly admitted it.

11. Sought through prayer and meditation to improve our conscious contact with God as we understood Him, praying only for knowledge of His will for us and the power to carry that out.

12. Having had a spiritual awakening as the result of these steps, we tried to carry this message to alcoholics and to practice these principles all our affairs.

From Alcoholic Anonymous, Copywright 19   . by Alcoholic Anonymous World Services, Inc. Reprinted by permission of Alcoholic Anonymous World Services, Inc.

FIG. 3-17   Twelve Steps to Alcoholics Anonymous

SUMMARY

Alcoholism and alcohol abuse represent a major public health problem that is not only epidemic in nature, but pandemic. The problem is not alcohol itself, but the people who use it. The problem will not go away by itself. Not only has the drug become a way of life in contemporary society, it is also part of our economy.

To date our educational programs have failed as evidenced by the magnitude of the problem and the fact that alcohol abuse is still surrounded by an array of misconceptions. This means that our present educational methods must be changed, intensified and scientifically applied. Prevention through education represents the best avenue to diminish the problem.

Common sense tells us that people will continue to use the drug. If this is the case, they must be educated to drink responsibly, and to recognize the early warning signs of alcoholism and alcohol abuse.

We need extensive research and rehabilitation programs, with cooperation from many disciplines. Educators, psychologists, sociologists, medical personnel, and religious leaders can all make valuable contributions.

Our experience with polio proves that an aroused public will pay the price to eliminate a serious health problem. Solving the problem of alcoholism and alcohol abuse will require a similar all-out effort.

BIBLIOGRAPHY (CHAPTER 3)

Alcoholics Anonymous World Services, Inc., *44 Questions and Answers About the A.A. Program of Recovery from Alcoholism.* New York, 1952.

BORKENSTEIN, R. F., R. F. CROWTHER, R. P. SHUMATE, W. B. ZIEL and R. ZYLMAN, *The Role of the Drinking Driver in Traffic Accidents*, 4th ed. Bloomington, Ind.: Department of Police Administration, Indiana University, 1963.

CARROLL, CHARLES C., *Alcohol: Use, Nonuse and Abuse.* Dubuque, Iowa: William C. Brown, 1970.

Distilled Spirits Council of the United States, Inc., *Facts Book: Public Attitudes and Economic Patterns.* Washington, D.C., 1974.

District of Columbia Alcoholic Rehabilitation Act of 1967, 90–452, Statute 618, 1968. See *Special Report No. 1435*, 90th Congress, 2nd Session, 1968.

FORT, JOEL, *Alcohol: Our Biggest Drug Problem.* New York: McGraw-Hill, 1973.

JELLINEK, E. M., *The Disease Concept of Alcoholism.* Highland Park, N.J.: Hillhouse Press, 1960.

LIEBER, CHARLES S., "Metabolic Effects Produced by Alcohol in the Liver and Other Tissues," ed. ISODORE SNAPPER and GENE H. STOLLERMAN. *Advances in Internal Medicine* 14 (1968):175.

MARDONES, JORGE, "The Alcohols," in *Physiological Pharmacology*, ed. WALTER S. ROOT and FREDERICK G. HOFFMAN. New York: Academic Free Press, 1963.

National Safety Council, *Accident Facts*, 1973 edition. Chicago, 1973.

OAKLEY, RAY S., *Drugs, Society and Human Behavior*, (rev. ed.). St. Louis, Mo.: C. V. Mosby, 1974.

RUBIN, EMANUEL, and CHARLES S. LIEBER, "Alcohol-Induced Hepatic Injury in Non Alcoholic Volunteers," *New England Journal of Medicine* 278 (1968): 869.

TERRIS, MILTON, "Epidemiology of Cirrhosis of the Liver: National Mortality Data," *American Journal of Public Health and the Nation's Health* 57 (1967): 2087.

United States Brewers Association, Inc., *United States Brewers Association: An American Tradition*. Washington, D.C., n.d.

United States Brewers Association, Inc., *The Brewers Almanac*. Washington, D.C., 1974.

United States Brewers Foundation, *Barley, Hops, and History*. New York, n.d.

U.S. Department of Health, Education and Welfare, *First Special Report to the U.S. Congress on Alcohol and Health*, ed. MARK KELLER, SHIRLEY S. ROSENBERG, et al. Washington, D.C., 1971.

VICTOR, MAURICE, and RAYMOND ADAMS, "On the Etiology of Alcoholic Neurological Diseases, with Special Reference to the Role of Nutrition," *The American Journal of Clinical Nutrition* 9 (1961).

WORICK, W. WAYNE, *Safety Education: Man, His Machines and His Environment*. Englewood Cliffs, N.J.: Prentice-Hall, 1975.

FOOTNOTES (CHAPTER 3)

[1]United States Brewers Foundation, *Barley, Hops, and History* (New York, n.d.), p. 2.

[2]*Ibid.*

[3]*Ibid.*

[4]*Ibid.*, pp. 3–5.

[5]United States Brewers Association, Inc., *United States Brewers Association: An American Tradition* (Washington, D.C., n.d.), p. 1.

[6]Distilled Spirits Council of the United States, Inc., *Facts Book: Public Attitudes and Economic Patterns* (Washington, D.C., 1974), p. 4.

[7]United States Brewers Association, Inc. *The Brewers Almanac* (Washington, D.C., 1974), p. 3.

[8]*Ibid.*, p. 4.

[9]Distilled Spirits Council, *op. cit.*, p. 25.

[10]United States Brewers Association,Inc. *The Brewers Almanac*, p. 4.

[11]U.S. Department of Health, Education and Welfare, *First Special Report to the U.S. Congress on Alcohol and Health*, ed. Mark Keller, Shirley S. Rosenberg, et al., (Washington, D.C., 1974), p. 35.

[12]*Ibid.*, p. 9.

[13]United States Brewers Association, Inc. *The Brewers Almanac*, p. 82.

[14]Ibid.

[15]U.S. Department of Health, Education and Welfare, op. cit., p. 27.

[16]Ibid.

[17]Ibid.

[18]Ibid.

[19]Jorge Mardones, "The Alcohols," in Physiological Pharmacology, ed. Walter S. Root and Frederick G. Hoffman (New York: Academic Free Press, 1963), p. 111.

[20]U.S. Department of Health, Education and Welfare, op. cit., p. 46.

[21]Charles R. Carroll, Alcohol: Use, Nonuse, and Abuse (Dubuque, Iowa: William C. Brown, 1970), p. 28.

[22]Oakley, S. Ray, Drugs, Society, and Human Behavior (updated 1974), (St. Louis, Mo.: The C. V. Mosby Co.), p. 89.

[23]Ibid., p. 87.

[24]National Safety Council, Accident Facts, 1975 Edition (Chicago, 1975), p. 97.

[25]U.S. Department of Health, Education and Welfare, op. cit., p. 39.

[26]W. Wayne Worick, Safety Education: Man, His Machines and His Environment (Englewood Cliffs, N.J.: Prentice-Hall, 1975), p. 12.

[27]National Safety Council, op. cit., p. 52.

[28]Worick, op. cit., p. 53.

[29]R. F. Borkenstein, R. F. Crowther, R. P. Shumate, W. B. Ziel, and R. Zylman, The Role of the Drinking Driver in Traffic Accidents, 4th ed. (Bloomington, Ind.: Department of Police Administration, Indiana University, 1963), p. 17.

[30]Ibid., p. xvii.

[31]Ibid.

[32]U.S. Department of Health, Education and Welfare, op. cit., p. 39.

[33]Ibid.

[34]Ibid.

[35]Ibid.

[36]Joel Fort, Alcohol: Our Biggest Drug Problem (New York: McGraw-Hill, 1973), p. 9.

[37]E. M. Jellinek, The Disease Concept of Alcoholism (Highland Park, N.J.: Hillhouse Press, 1960), pp. 35–38.

[38]Fort, op. cit., p. viii.

[39]District of Columbia Alcoholic Rehabilitation Act of 1967, P.L. 90–452, Statute 618, (1968).

[40]U.S. Department of Health, Education and Welfare, op. cit., p. 45.

[41]Ibid.

[42]Maurice Victor and Raymond Adams, "On the Etiology of Alcoholic Neurological Diseases with Special Reference to the Role of Nutrition," The American Journal of Clinical Nutrition 9 (1961), p. 393.

[43]Emanuel Rubin and Charles S. Lieber, "Alcohol-Induced Hepatic Injury in Non-Alcoholic Volunteers," Reprinted by Permission from the *New England Journal of Medicine* 278 (1968), p. 869.

[44]From Charles S. Lieber, "Metabolic Effects Produced by Alcohol in the Liver and Other Tissues," in Isodore Snapper and Gene H. Stollerman (eds.), *Advances in Internal Medicine*, Vol. 14., copyright 1968 by Year Book Medical Publishers, Inc. Used by permission.

[45]U.S. Department of Health, Education and Welfare, *op. cit.*, p. 47.

[46]Milton Terris, "Epidemiology of Cirrhosis of the Liver: National Mortality Data," *American Journal of Public Health and the Nation's Health* 57 (1967), p. 2087.

[47]U.S. Department of Health, Education and Welfare, *op. cit.*, p. 48.

[48]From *44 Questions and Answers About the A.A. Program of Recovery from Alcoholism*, copyright 1952 by Alcoholics Anonymous World Services, Inc., p. 14. Reprinted by permission of Alcoholics Anonymous World Services, Inc.

[49]From *Alcoholics Anonymous*, copyright 1955, by Alcoholics Anonymous World Services, Inc., pp. 59–60. Reprinted by permission of Alcoholics Anonymous World Services, Inc.

four

SMOKING AND HEALTH

There is, perhaps, no other personal health behavior that has received greater attention from the media than smoking. Smoking cigarettes, cigars or a pipe has been depicted as being any one, and sometimes more than one of the following: masculine, feminine, young, mature, sensual, sexy, affluent, sporty, etc., etc. Notwithstanding these advertising images, in 1964 the Surgeon General's Report on *Smoking and Health* officially described smoking as being hazardous to one's health.[1]

Tobacco was used by the American Indians for its medicinal value. After his adventures in the New World, Sir Walter Raleigh took tobacco back to England, where he promoted pipe-smoking, chewing and snuffing of tobacco. It was even praised for its medicinal value. Cigarette smoking seldom occurred until World War I when free cigarettes were given to service men. Smoking of tobacco leaves wrapped in paper as small cigars started in Spain and then quickly spread throughout Europe, and in a relatively short time, tobacco use became world-wide.

Cigar smoking lost its popularity between 1920 and 1930 because of the increased popularity of cigarette smoking. Cigarette smoking in the United States was not common before World War I. Since World War I cigar smoking has maintained its rather low profile and low rate of consumption, but cigarette smoking has increased to over four times the number consumed in 1925.[2]

For all practical purposes smoking by women was unknown until the 1920's. Independence and the desire to do as men did were some of the reasons women began to smoke. Advertising also played a major part—it indicated that romance, independence, glamour and social success were the results of using a particular brand of cigarette. Statistics for females are rapidly becoming equal to those for males in terms of morbidity and mortality attributed to smoking.

Smoking and its potential deleterious effect on the human body has long been suspected, if not recognized as a problem. For example, tobacco and its effect on health have been studied for over one hundred years. In 1859 a French physician reported in a retrospective study of 68 cases of oral cancer that 66 individuals smoked tobacco and one chewed tobacco.[3]

Cigarette smoking is a major world-wide problem today, and reduction in tobacco consumption is a world-wide goal as stated by conferees at several world conferences on smoking and health. There has been a recent small decline in consumption as a result of public reports of the dangers associated with cigarette smoking, but in countries where extensive advertising and other types of promotion occur, it has been difficult to reduce smoking.

EFFECTS OF SMOKING ON THE HUMAN BODY

Since smokers have a higher mortality rate than nonsmokers, the question arises as to what physical changes occur within the body when one smokes. Unfortunately not all the answers are known. Figure 4-1 will test your knowledge and understanding of the respiratory system and the effect of smoking on it. It may be necessary for you to review other sources for answers to these questions. See bibliography for suggested resources.

In just three seconds a cigarette makes your heart beat faster, raises your blood pressure, replaces oxygen in your blood with carbon monoxide and leaves cancer-causing chemicals to traumatize various body organs. All this happens each time you smoke and the damage adds up. Figure 4-2 dramatizes the immediate effects of smoking on the human body.

Smoking also narrows the blood vessels that supply the skin. This is especially true in the skin of the fingers and toes. This added constriction is especially harmful if the person already has

RESPIRATORY SYSTEM AND SMOKING KNOWLEDGE TEST

CIRCLE THE CORRECT ANSWER TO THE FOLLOWING QUESTIONS.

1, THE LEADING CAUSE OF DEATH IN THE UNITED STATES TODAY IS: (A) CANCER; (B) EMPHYSEMA; (C) HEART DISEASE; (D) BRONCHITIS.

2. THE PROCESS OF GAS EXCHANGE WITHIN THE AIR SACS IS CALLED: (A) DIFFUSION; (B) FUSION; (C) RESPIRATION; (D) OSMOSIS.

3. THE TERM METASTASIZE USUALLY IS USED WITH: (A) LUNG CANCER; (B) EMPHYSEMA; (C) BRONCHITIS; (D) ASTHMA.

4. DIASTOLE AND SYSTOLE DESCRIBES: (A) BLOOD PRESSURE; (B) RESPIRATION RATE; (C) NERVOUS IMPULSES; (D) NONE OF THE ABOVE.

5. MAN NEEDS ABOUT_____POUNDS OF AIR A DAY TO EXIST: (A) 15;(B) 25; (C) 35; (D) 45.

6. WHAT SUBSTANCE IS NOT IN CIGARETTE SMOKE: (A) AMMONIA; (B) NICOTINE; (C) ACETALDEHYDE; (D) XYLENE.

7. THE TERMINAL BRONCHIOLES ARE_____IN DIAMETER: (A) 1/2 in.; (B) 1/4 in.; (C) 1/10 in.; (D) 1/100 in.

8. EMPHYSEMA IS CHARACTERIZED BEST BY: (A) CHEST PAIN, COUGHING-UP BLOOD; (B) SORE THROAT, SHORTNESS OF BREATH; (C) SHORTNESS OF BREATH DUE TO OVER-INFLATION OF AIR SPACES; (D) SHALLOW BREATHING, CHEST PAIN.

9. HUMAN LUNGS ARE COMPOSED OF HOW MANY ALVEOLI: (A) 100 MILLION; (B) 350 MILLION; (C) 600 MILLION; (D) 750 MILLION.

10. WHAT ARE THE TWO TYPES OF BRONCHITIS: (A) ACUTE AND CHRONIC; (B) BENIGN AND MALIGNANT; (C) LATENT AND ACTIVE; (D) NONE OF THE ABOVE.

11. THE BEST WAY TO DESCRIBE THE LUNG IS: (A) LAYER AFTER LAYER OF SMOOTH MUSCLE; (B) LAYER AFTER LAYER OF SPONGY ELASTIC TISSUE; (C) LAYER AFTER LAYER OF COARSE DARK TISSUE; (D) LAYER AFTER LAYER OF BROWN SPONGY TISSUE.

12. A PREGNANT WOMAN WHO SMOKES RISKS: (A) STILLBIRTHS; (B) LOW WEIGHT BABY; (C) SPONTANEOUS ABORTIONS; (D) ALL OF THE ABOVE.

13. THE WALL S OF THE TINY AIR SACS OF THE LUNGS ARE SURROUNDED BY A NETWORK OF: (A) VESSELS; (B) ARTERIES; (C) NERVES; (D) CAPILLARIES.

FIG. 4-1 Respiratory System and Smoking Knowledge Test (Source: Brady, Dale, E., *The Respiratory System and Smoking*, Chicago Lung Association, 1973. *Reprinted by permission of The Chicago Lung Association.*)

14. WHAT EFFECT DOES SMOKING HAVE ON THE VASCULAR SYSTEM: (A) INCREASES HEART RATE AND BLOOD PRESSURE; (B) INCREASES HEART RATE AND DECREASES BLOOD PRESSURE; (C) DECREASES HEART RATE AND INCREASES BLOOD PRESSURE; (D) DECREASES HEART RATE AND BLOOD PRESSURE.

15. VITAL CAPACITY IS: (A) THE VOLUME OF AIR THAT OCCURS DURING NORMAL BREATHING; (B) TOTAL AMOUNT OF AIR LEFT IN THE LUNGS AFTER EXPIRATION; (C) TOTAL AMOUNT OF AIR ONE LUNG CAN HOLD; (D) TOTAL VOLUME OF THE MAXIMUM AMOUNT OF AIR THAT CAN BE INHALED AND EXHALED.

16. IN LUNG CANCER, CELL CHANGES IN THE EPITHELIUM OF THE AIR PASSAGES BEGINS WITH AN INCREASE IN THE NUMBER OF: (A) SQUAMOUS CELLS; (B) COLUMNAR CELLS; (C) BASAL CELLS; (D) SURFACE CELLS.

17. WHICH GROUP IS IN THE CORRECT ANATOMICAL ORDER: (A) TRACHEA, BRONCHIOLE, BRONCHI, ALVEOLI; (B) ALVEOLI, TRACHEA, BRONCHI, BRONCHIOLE; (C) TRACHEA, BRONCHI, BRONCHIOLE, ALVEOLI; (D) BRONCHI, TRACHEA, BRONCHIOLE, ALVEOLI.

18. SECOND-HAND SMOKE AFFECTS: (A) A NON-SMOKER; (B) A PERSON WITH BRONCHOPULMONARY DISEASE; (C) A PERSON WITH CORONARY HEART DISEASE; (D) ALL PEOPLE.

19. THE WALLS OF THE ALVEOLI ARE CALLED: (A) PLEURA; (B) SEPTA; (C) CILIA; (D) EPITHELIUM.

20. CANCER CAN BE BEST DEFINED AS: (A) A CHRONIC CONDITION; (B) A FATAL DISEASE; (C) ERRATIC GROWTH OF CELLS; (C) A DISEASE WITH SPECIFIC SYMPTOMS.

21. THE RESPIRATORY SYSTEM IS CONTROLLED BY THE PART OF THE BRAIN CALLED THE: (A) MEDULLA OBLONGATA; (B) CEREBELLUM; (C) CEREBRUM; (D) THALMUS.

22. HEART ATTACKS IN SMOKERS, AS COMPARED TO NON-SMOKERS, ARE: (A) NO DIFFERENT; (B) TWICE AS HIGH; (C) TWO TO THREE TIMES AS HIGH; (D) THREE TO FOUR TIMES AS HIGH.

23. THE "STREET SWEEPERS" OF THE LUNGS REFER TO THE: (A) MUCUS MAKING CELLS; (B) CILIA; (C) EPITHELIAL CELLS; (D) BLOOD CELLS.

24. UNTIL TOLERANCE IS DEVELOPED, WHAT EFFECT DOES SMOKING HAVE ON THE CENTRAL NERVOUS SYSTEM: (A) COUGHING; (B) NAUSEA; (C) DIZZINESS; (D) BOTH B AND C.

Fig. 4-1 (Cont'd.)

25. WHAT ARTERIES SUPPLY THE HEART WITH OXYGEN AND NUTRIENTS: (A) PULMONARY; (B) VENA CAVA; (C) CORONARY; (D) AORTA.

26. BRONCHITIS IS FIRST CHARACTERIZED BY: (A) CHEST PAIN; (B) COUGHING; (C) SPITTING UP BLOOD; (D) SPOTS ON THE LUNG.

27. THE HUMAN HEART IS STRENGTHENED THROUGH: (A) EXERCISE; (B) RESTING; (C) SMOKING; (D) SLEEPING.

28. SMOKING DOES ALL THE FOLLOWING EXCEPT: (A) CONSTRICT THE BLOOD VESSELS; (B) INCREASE THE HEART RATE; (C) DECREASE THE RESPIRATORY RATE; (D) INCREASE THE BLOOD PRESSURE.

29. A TYPICAL BLOOD PRESSURE FOR A YOUNG ADULT IS: (A) 150/90; (B) 140/90; (C) 130/80; (D) 120/80.

30. NICOTINE INTRODUCED INTO THE MOTHER'S BLOOD STREAM IMPAIRS ALL BUT THE UNBORN BABY'S: (A) HEART RATE; (B)WATER BALANCE; (C) BLOOD PRESSURE; (D) OXYGEN SUPPLY.

31. THE MOST PREVENTABLE CAUSE OF DEATH TODAY IS: (A) OVERWEIGHT; (B) SMOKING; (C) BACTERIAL INFECTIONS; (D)POOR NUTRITION.

32. _____DIFFUSES 20 TO 30 TIMES FASTER THAN OXYGEN: (A) CARBON DIOXIDE; (B) NITROGEN DIOXIDE; (C) SULFUR DIOXIDE; (D) CARBON MONIXIDE.

33. WHICH DISEASE DOES SOCIAL SECURITY PAY MORE IN BENEFITS: (A) EMPHYSEMA; (B) LUNG CANCER; (C) BRONCHITIS; (D) ASTHMA.

34. LUNG CANCER USUALLY BEGINS WITH CHANGES IN THE GROWTH PATTERN OF THE CELLS IN THE: (A) ALVEOLI; (B) TRACHEA; (C) BRONCHIAL TREE; (D) PLEURA.

35. THE MAIN MUSCLE(S) OF RESPIRATION: (A) RIB MUSCLES; (B) DIAPHRAGM; (C) ABDOMINAL MUSCLES; (D) OBLIQUES EXTERNUS ABDOMINIS.

36. ARTEROSCLEROSIS IS: (A) HEART ATTACK; (B) HARDENING OF THE ARTERIES; (C) SCAR TISSUE OF THE HEART; (D) FATTY SUBSTANCES IN THE BLOOD.

37. BRONCHOGENIC CARCINOMA IS THE MOST COMMON TYPE OF: (A) LUNG CANCER; (B) HEART DISEASE; (C) BRONCHITIS; (D) EMPHYSEMA.

Fig. 4-1 (Cont'd.)

38. CIGARETTE SMOKING CAN CAUSE WHAT DISEASE BY ITS RESTRICTION OF THE FLOW OF BLOOD TO THE FINGERS AND TOES: (A) HUNTINGTON'S CHOREA; (B) HODGKIN'S DISEASE; (C) BUERGER'S DISEASE; (D) VENEREAL DISEASE.

39. WHICH PART OF THE BLOOD CARRIES OXYGEN: (A) PLASMA; (B) HEMOGLOBIN; (C) WHITE BLOOD CELLS; (D) MACROPHAGES.

40. WHAT IS THE MAJOR CAUSE OF LUNG CANCER: (A) SMOKING: (B) AIR POLLUTION; (C) RADIATION; (D) GENES.

41. WHICH RISK FACTORS ARE NOT ASSOCIATED WITH HEART DISEASE: (A) HYPERTENSION; (B) DIABETES; (C) UNDERWEIGHT; (D) SMOKING.

42. WHAT VESSEL CARRIES THE DEOXYGENATED BLOOD TO THE LUNGS: (A) PULMONARY VEIN; (B) PULMONARY ARTERY; (C) CORONARY ARTERY; (D) CORONARY VEIN.

43. EMPHYSEMA IS BEST DESCRIBED BY ALL THE FOLLOWING EXCEPT: (A) OVER INFLATION OF THE AIR SACS; (B) DESTRUCTION OF THE AIR SAC WALLS; (C) LOWERED OXYGEN IN THE BLOOD; (D) DEFLATION OF THE AIR SACS.

44. THE THIN MEMBRANE THAT LINES EACH HALF OF THE CHEST CAVITY AND ENVELOPES THE LUNGS IS THE: (A) BASAL MEMBRANE; (B) DIAPHRAGM; (C) INTERCOSTALS; (D) PLEURA.

45. CHRONIC BRONCHITIS IS BEST CHARACTERIZED BY ALL BUT: (A) INFLAMMATION OF THE LINING OF THE BRONCHIAL TUBES; (B) MUCUS GLANDS OVER-PRODUCE; (C) DESTRUCTION OF ALVEOLI WALLS; (D) MUCUS PLUGS.

46. BOTH MEN AND WOMEN SMOKERS HAVE HIGHER DEATH RATES FROM STROKE IN THE AGE GROUP FROM: (A) 45-74; (B) 35-65; (C) 60-75; (D) 50-74.

47. THE FIRST SYMPTOMS OF LUNG CANCER MAY BE ALL EXCEPT: (A) COUGHING; (B) DIZZINESS; (C) SHORTNESS OF BREATH; (D) INCREASED EXPECTORATION.

48. WHAT TYPE OF CELLS LINE THE AIR PASSAGES: (A) CILIATES SQUAMOUS EPITHELIAL CELLS; (B) CILIATED BASAL EPITHELIAL CELLS; (C) CILIATED COLUMNAR EPITHELIAL CELLS; (D) NONE OF THE ABOVE.

49. LUNGS OF EMPHYSEMATOUS PATIENTS ARE CHARACTERIZED BY THE FOLLOWING EXCEPT: (A) GROSSLY ENLARGED; (B) WHITER THAN NORMAL LUNGS; (C) DOWNY IN TEXTURE; (D) SMALLER THAN NORMAL.

50. THE CHRISTMAS SEAL PEOPLE ARE CONCERNED ABOUT: (A) LUNG CANCER; (B) EMPHYSEMA; (C) BRONCHITIS; (D) ALL LUNG DISEASES.

Fig. 4-1 (Cont'd.)

**Listen Smokers:
You don't have to wait 20 years
for cigarettes to affect you.
It only takes 3 seconds.**

In just 3 seconds a cigarette makes your heart beat faster,
shoots your blood pressure up, replaces oxygen in your blood with
carbon monoxide, and leaves cancer-causing chemicals
to spread through your body.
All this happens with every cigarette you smoke.
As the cigarettes add up, the damage adds up.
Because it's the cumulative effects of smoking—adding this
cigarette to all the cigarettes you ever smoked—
that causes the trouble.
And tell that to your dog, too.

FIG. 4-2 The Effects of Smoking Are Immediate and Hazardous
(Source: U. S. Department of Health, Education and Welfare.)

peripheral vascular disease, thus complicating this disease process. Smoking for such an individual increases the risk of gangrene, amputation and even death, although actual cases are quite rare.

Figures 4-3 and 4-4 describe the respiratory system. When a smoker puffs on a cigarette, smoke remains inside the mouth and can travel into the throat and windpipe. It travels into the upper breathing passages and is swallowed after becoming dissolved in the saliva. Smoke is also absorbed by the mucous membranes of the mouth.

After smoke passes through the mouth, the lungs retain 85–99 percent of all compounds inhaled. Of the hundreds of such compounds, among the most damaging are tar, carbon monoxide and hydrogen cyanide. Hydrogen cyanide is a powerful poison and,

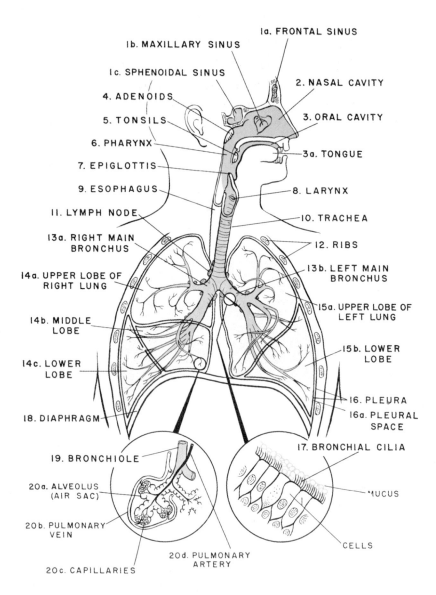

FIG. 4-3 Physiology of the Respiratory System (*Courtesy of The American Lung Association.*)

along with the other gases, attenuates the cleansing effectiveness of the cilia in removing foreign particles. Thus, cells and tissues are vulnerable to these irritants.

THE RESPIRATORY SYSTEM

This chart of the RESPIRATORY SYSTEM shows the apparatus for breathing. Breathing is the process by which oxygen in the air is brought into the lungs and into close contact with the blood, which absorbs it and carries it to all parts of the body. At the same time the blood gives up waste matter (carbon dioxide), which is carried out of the lungs with the air breathed out.

1. The SINUSES (Frontal, Maxillary, and Sphenoidal) are hollow spaces in the bones of the head. Small openings connect them to the nasal cavity. The functions they serve are not clearly understood, but include helping to regulate the temperature and humidity of air breathed in, as well as to lighten the bone structure of the head and to give resonance to the voice.

2. The NASAL CAVITY (nose) is the preferred entrance for outside air into the Respiratory System. The hairs that line the inside wall are part of the air-cleansing system.

3. Air also enters through the ORAL CAVITY (mouth), especially in people who have a mouth-breathing habit or whose nasal passages may be temporarily obstructed, as by a cold.

4. The ADENOIDS are overgrown lymph tissue at the top of the throat. When they interfere with breathing, they are generally removed. The lymph system, consisting of nodes (knots of cells) and connecting vessels, carries fluid throughout the body. This system helps to resist body infection by filtering out foreign matter, including germs, and producing cells (lymphocytes) to fight them.

5. The TONSILS are lymph nodes in the wall of the pharynx that often become infected. They are an unimportant part of the germ-fighting system of the body. When infected, they are generally removed.

6. The PHARYNX (throat) collects incoming air from the nose and mouth and passes it downward to the trachea (windpipe).

7. The EPIGLOTTIS is a flap of tissue that guards the entrance to the trachea, closing when anything is swallowed that should go into the esophagus and stomach.

8. The LARYNX (voice box) contains the vocal cords. It is the place where moving air being breathed in and out creates voice sounds.

9. The ESOPHAGUS is the passage leading from mouth and throat to the stomach.

10. The TRACHEA (windpipe) is the passage leading from the pharynx to the lungs.

11. The LYMPH NODES of the lungs are found against the walls of the bronchial tubes and trachea.

12. The RIBS are bones supporting and protecting the chest cavity. They move to a limited degree, helping the lungs to expand and contract.

13. The trachea divides into the two main BRONCHI (tubes), one for each lung, which subdivide into the lobar bronchi—three on the right and two on the left. These, in turn, subdivide further.

14. The right lung is divided into three LOBES, or sections. Each lobe is like a balloon filled with sponge-like lung tissue. Air moves in and out through one opening—a branch of the bronchus.

15. The left lung is divided into two LOBES.

16. The PLEURA are the two membranes, actually one continuous one folded on itself, that surround each lobe of the lungs and separate the lungs from the chest wall.

17. The bronchial tubes are lined with CILIA (like very small hairs) that have a wave-like motion. This motion carries MUCUS (sticky phlegm or liquid) upward and out into the throat, where it is either coughed up or swallowed. The mucus catches and holds much of the dust, germs, and other unwanted matter that has invaded the lungs and thus gets rid of it.

18. The DIAPHRAGM is the strong wall of muscle that separates the chest cavity from the abdominal cavity. By moving downward, it creates suction to draw in air and expand the lungs.

19. The smallest subdivisions of the bronchi are called BRONCHIOLES, at the end of which are the alveoli (plural of alveolus).

20. The ALVEOLI are the very small air sacs that are the destination of air breathed in. The CAPILLARIES are blood vessels that are imbedded in the walls of the alveoli. Blood passes through the capillaries, brought to them by the PULMONARY ARTERY and taken away by the PULMONARY VEIN. While in the capillaries the blood discharges carbon dioxide into the alveoli and takes up oxygen from the air in the alveoli.

A Christmas Seal service of

YOUR ✚ LUNG ASSOCIATION

Published by AMERICAN LUNG ASSOCIATION, formerly National Tuberculosis and Respiratory Disease Association

FIG. 4-4 The Respiratory System (*Courtesy of The American Lung Association.*)

Carbon monoxide combines with hemoglobin in the blood cells to reduce the oxygen-carrying capacity of the cells. The levels of carbon monoxide gas in smokers' blood is up to four times the normal amount. Heavy smokers may have levels 15 times the normal carbon monoxide level.

The reduced oxygen-carrying capacity is normally associated with aging. Scientists at the University of Florida compared blood from smokers under 40 with blood from nonsmokers 60–70 years old. It was found the blood samples were the same as far as oxygen-carrying ability was concerned. This kind of aging is reversible; if a person quits smoking, the oxygen-carrying ability will return to normal.[4]

Smoking causes decreased oxygen flow to the retina resulting in loss of visual acuity and color perception for some people. There may be decreased sensitivity, particularly at night.

It is the nicotine in the tar that causes the blood vessels to constrict thereby reducing the flow of blood and oxygen to some parts of the body. The heart then has to pump harder.

In addition to nicotine, tar contains several hundred chemicals including about twelve that produce cancer in animals. Experiments have shown that mice develop cancer of the skin when repeatedly exposed to diluted solutions of the tar. Some of the chemicals in tobacco tar do not produce cancer by themselves but only when they interact with other chemicals, thus stimulating the growth of certain cancers.

Tar damages the lung tissue; when the tiny particles of tar cool inside the lung they produce a brown sticky mass. This mass contains the cancer-causing chemicals. Tobacco tar stops ciliary action and, eventually, the cilia are destroyed. Cilia act to cause mucous to flow up and out of the lungs and when mucous membranes surrounding the cilia are destroyed the mucous must be brought up by coughing. Various studies clearly demonstrate that cigarette filters are ineffective in removing tars, see Figure 4-5.

Smoking does have an effect on fatigue. Nicotine causes a temporary increase in production of sugar, resulting in more fuel for body muscles. After the sugar is used up, fatigue returns and the feeling of tiredness is greater than before. Smoking may relax the nervous tension caused by craving a cigarette, but there is no evidence that cigarette smoking has any other tranquilizing effects.

Studies show that nicotine or cigarette smoking stimulates the adrenal glands to produce an increased amount of hormone which alters other organs and glands. One study at Philadelphia General

even
the
longest
filter
doesn't
help
much!

FIG. 4-5 Cigarette Filters Are Not Effective in Reducing Tar Damage to Lung Tissue (Source: *U. S. Department of Health, Education and Welfare.*)

Hospital indicated a 27 to 77 percent increase in the amount of adrenal hormones after subjects smoked normally for 30 minutes.[5] Controls showed a decline in hormones which normally vary during the day. There was no suggestion as to what effect this hormone rise might have on health, but any unnatural change in normal amounts of hormones could be harmful.

A beginning smoker shows signs of nicotine poisoning. Symptoms include dizziness, rapid pulse, cold clammy skin and sometimes nausea and diarrhea. These symptoms are a result of the immediate effects of nicotine on the central nervous autonomic nervous systems. Nausea results when nicotine affects the vomiting center. The dizziness and unsteadiness result when the equilibrium maintenance center of the brain is affected. All these symptoms diminish as tolerance to the nicotine is developed.

For the beginner, the most obvious effect of nicotine is a short-term stimulation followed by depression of both sympathetic and central nervous systems. Nicotine causes a discharge of epinephrine from the adrenal glands. This in turn stimulates the nervous system and other endocrine glands and causes the liver to release glycogen (sugar). The result is a feeling of stimulation or "kick" and a relief of fatigue. This is only short-term, and is followed by depression and further fatigue. Various investigators think that nicotine is the addictive ingredient of tobacco.

SMOKING STATISTICS

Who smokes? Forty-three percent of adult men and 31 percent of adult women are regular smokers. Millions have given up the habit. At one time in their lives, 75 percent of the male population and 46 percent of the female population have smoked. Men as a group smoke more—26 percent smoke more than one pack a day, as do 18 percent of women. For both sexes, 15–24 cigarettes per day is the most common number smoked. The highest proportion of smokers of both sexes is in the age group 24–44 years.[6]

Another way to view tobacco consumption is by pounds of tobacco consumed. There has been a steady increase in the pounds of tobacco consumed per person age 15 and over during the first 50 years of this century. In 1900, 7.42 pounds of tobacco for all purposes were consumed per person. This included 49 cigarettes per person, age 15 and over. In 1950 a peak of 11.59 pounds was reached. Since 1950, total poundage of tobacco consumed has declined but the number of cigarettes has increased from 3,322 to 4,003 per person. The per capita consumption of cigarettes continues to increase as does the total manufacture of cigarettes.

Mortality

A two-pack-a-day smoker smokes three-quarters of a million cigarettes during his lifetime. As a result, he loses 8.3 years or 4.4 million minutes of his life. This amounts to a loss of almost 6 minutes per cigarette smoked, or a minute of life lost for a minute of smoking.

Many prospective studies[7,8,9] have indicated that the mortality rate for cigarette smokers is greater than for nonsmokers or for cigar and pipe smokers. Regardless of age, the mortality rate is 30–80 percent higher for smokers than nonsmokers. It should be noted that the chance of mortality still increases with increased cigar consumption. The mortality of cigarette smokers is greater at ages 45–54 than in younger or older age groups.

In a study for the American Cancer Society, Hammond and

Horn support the findings of the above three studies.[10] To quote the findings as cited by Diehl:[11]

> The most important findings of the study were that the total death rate from all causes combined, is far higher among cigarette smokers than among nonsmokers or pipe and cigar smokers and that the death rate increases in direct relation to the number of cigarettes smoked.

Other conclusions concerning the over-all death rate were as follows:

> Death rates of both men and women were higher among subjects with a history of cigarette smoking than among those who never smoked regularly. Death rate of current cigarette smokers increased with the number of cigarettes smoked per day and the degree of inhalation.
>
> Death rates were higher among current cigarette smokers who started the habit at a young age than among those who started later in life. Among both men and women, the difference between the death rates of cigarette smokers and nonsmokers increases with age. Among men, the death rate for ex-cigarette smokers was lower than for men smoking cigarettes when they enrolled in the study. The death rate of ex-cigarette smokers decreased with the length of time since they last smoked cigarettes.
>
> Total death rates and death rates from most of the common diseases occurring in both sexes were higher for men than for women, higher for men who never smoked regularly than for women who never smoked regularly, and far higher for men who were regular cigarette smokers than for women who smoked regularly. Among both men and women, death rates from the following diseases were much higher in cigarette smokers than in nonsmokers: Emphysema; cancer of the lungs; cancer of the buccal cavity (i.e., tissue inside the mouth); cancer of the pharynx, larynx, and esophagus; aortic aneurysm; and cancer of the pancreas.
>
> Death rates from coronary heart disease and from stroke also were significantly higher—about twice as high—for both men and women who smoked than for nonsmokers.[12]

Cost to Health

A high-risk smoker is one who is more susceptible, for example, to lung cancer. However, smoking may be harmful to any individual. It was estimated that in 1967, 300,000 deaths were attributed to smoking. In daily figures, 800 deaths a day in the U.S. are related to cigarette smoking. Of these, 175 a day are due to cancer, 375 a day to diseases of the heart and circulatory system, and 250 a day to chronic bronchitis, emphysema, peptic ulcers and other diseases.[13]

Smoking also reduces the length of life, in direct relation to number of cigarettes smoked. The life expectancy of a man 25 years of age is reduced by 4.6 years if he smokes less than a half a pack of cigarettes a day; by 5.5 years if he smokes one-half to 1 pack a day; by 6.2 years if he smokes 1 to 2 packs a day and by 8.3 years if he smokes 2 or more packs a day.[14]

Unfortunately the identification of high-risk smokers cannot yet be done. Warning signs include a smoker's cough or evidence of abnormal lung function. Smoking is contraindicated if one has symptoms indicating increased risk of coronary heart disease. Pregnant women are vulnerable, as are their fetuses. Smoking is harmful to persons with gastric or duodenal ulcers.

SMOKING AND CANCER

Initial concern about the potential effects of smoking began when scientists searched for a reason for the increasing death rate from lung cancer. Early studies linked smoking and lung cancer. However, it was later determined that only a small amount of the excess overall mortality found among smokers could be attributed to lung cancer. It was found that the rest was largely due to coronary heart disease, chronic respiratory disease and other forms of cancer. It was also found that the effect on overall mortality was restricted to cigarette smokers rather than the users of other forms of tobacco.

Lung Cancer

Cigarette smoking has been clearly identified as a cause of lung cancer. This conclusion is based on more than 20 years of research. For both men and women the risk of developing lung cancer depends on the number of cigarettes smoked per day, number of cigarettes smoked in a lifetime, the number of years smoked, the age of first smoking, the depth of inhalation of smoke and the tar and nicotine levels of the cigarette.[15]

A recent World Health Organization report revealed that the cancer rate for women is slightly lower than for men. However, as women smokers smoke more, their lung cancer death rates are increasing. Increased exposure may have been altered by the ten-

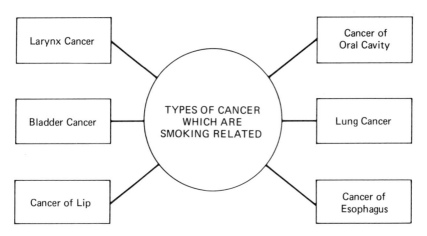

FIG. 4-6   Types of Cancer Related to Smoking

dency of women to smoke filter-tip cigarettes, which have lower tar content.[16]

Those who stop smoking have a lowered risk of dying from lung cancer, but it is still higher than the risk for nonsmokers. Air pollution has been shown to result in higher lung cancer death rates, but the effect is relatively small compared to the effect produced by cigarette smoking.

There is evidence that on cessation of smoking the epithelial abnormalities commonly found in the bronchi of cigarette smokers regress and the bronchial epithelium is as free of atypical cells as that of nonsmokers. This provides evidence that lung cancer rates for smokers decline after they cease to smoke.

In a British study of doctors, a striking reduction occurred in lung cancer deaths after smokers quit smoking, whereas the rate of lung cancer in the general population continued to rise as the public did little to change their smoking habits. This indicates that a widespread cessation of smoking would rapidly reduce lung cancer mortality.[17] Tables 4-1, 4-2 and 4-3 provide some statistics which describe the overall cancer problem. Study of these tables will give some perspective on the contribution of smoking to the total cancer problem.

Certain occupations are associated with increased risk of lung cancer. Cigarette smoking interacts with many of these risk factors. This interaction may be experienced simultaneously or at different times. The uranium mining and asbestos industries are examples of occupations where the increased risk occurs because of inter-action.[18]

Table 4-1. How to Estimate Cancer Statistics Locally

Community Population	Estimated No. Who are Alive, Cured of Cancer	Estimated No. Cancer Cases Under Medical Care in 1976	Estimated No. Who Will Die of Cancer in 1976	Estimated No. of New Cases in 1976	Estimated No. Who Will be Saved from Cancer in 1976	Estimated No. Who Will Eventually Develop Cancer	Estimated No. Who Will Die of Cancer if Present Rates Continue
1,000	7	4	1	3	1	250	150
2,000	15	9	3	6	2	500	300
3,000	22	13	4	8	3	750	450
4,000	30	18	6	11	4	1,000	600
5,000	37	21	7	14	5	1,250	750
10,000	74	43	15	28	9	2,500	1,500
25,000	185	107	37	70	23	6,250	3,750
50,000	370	215	75	140	47	12,500	7,500
100,000	740	430	150	280	93	25,000	15,000
200,000	1,480	860	300	560	186	50,000	30,000
500,000	3,700	2,150	750	1,400	465	125,000	75,000

NOTE: The figures can only be the roughest approximation of actual data for your community. It is suggested that every effort be made to obtain actual data from a Registry source.

SOURCE: Courtesy of American Cancer Society, Inc., '76 *Cancer Facts and Figures*, National Headquarters, American Cancer Society, New York, 1975.

Table 4-2a. Estimated New Cases and Deaths for Major Sites of Cancer – 1976*

Site	No. of Cases	Deaths
Lung	93,000	84,000
Colon-Rectum	99,000	49,000
Breast	89,000	33,000
Uterus	47,000**	11,000
Oral	24,000	8,000
Skin	9,000***	5,000
Leukemia	21,000	15,000

*Figures rounded to the nearest 1,000.

**If carcinoma-in-situ included, cases total over 86,000.

***Estimate new cases of non-melanoma about 300,000.

Incidence rates are based on rates from N.C.I. third national cancer survey 1969-71.

SOURCE: Courtesy of American Cancer Society, Inc. '76 *Cancer FACTS AND FIGURES*, National Headquarters, American Cancer Society, New York, 1975.

Table 4-2b. Five Year Cancer Survival Rates* for Selected Sites

Site	Localized	Regional Involvement
BLADDER	71%	21%
BREAST	84%	56%
COLON-RECTUM	71%	43%
LARYNX	79%	38%
LUNG	33%	10%
ORAL	67%	30%
PROSTATE	68%	57%
UTERUS	82%	44%

*Adjusted for normal life expectancy.

SOURCE: End Results Group, National Cancer Institute

Table 4-3a. Cancer Incidence and Deaths by Site and Sex

Table 4-3b. Cancer Deaths by Site and Sex

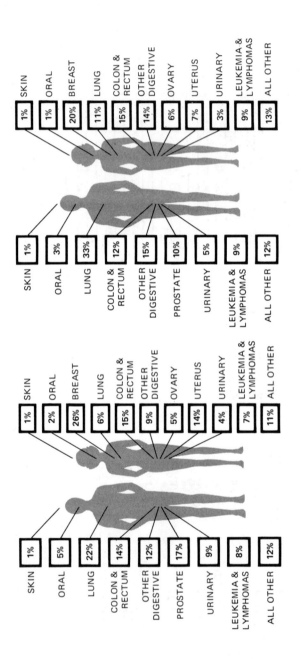

Table 4-3a (left):

SKIN 1%
ORAL 2%
BREAST 26%
LUNG 6%
COLON & RECTUM 15%
OTHER DIGESTIVE 9%
OVARY 5%
UTERUS 14%
URINARY 4%
LEUKEMIA & LYMPHOMAS 7%
ALL OTHER 11%

SKIN 1%
ORAL 5%
LUNG 22%
COLON & RECTUM 14%
OTHER DIGESTIVE 12%
PROSTATE 17%
URINARY 9%
LEUKEMIA & LYMPHOMAS 8%
ALL OTHER 12%

Table 4-3b (right):

SKIN 1%
ORAL 1%
BREAST 20%
LUNG 11%
COLON & RECTUM 15%
OTHER DIGESTIVE 14%
OVARY 6%
UTERUS 7%
URINARY 3%
LEUKEMIA & LYMPHOMAS 9%
ALL OTHER 13%

SKIN 1%
ORAL 3%
LUNG 33%
COLON & RECTUM 12%
OTHER DIGESTIVE 15%
PROSTATE 10%
URINARY 5%
LEUKEMIA & LYMPHOMAS 9%
ALL OTHER 12%

SOURCE: Courtesy of American Cancer Society, Inc., "76 *CANCER FACTS AND FIGURES*, National Headquarters, American Cancer Society, New York, 1975. (1976 estimates)

*Excluding non-melanoma skin cancer and carcinoma-in-situ of uterine cervix.

Lung cancer develops only in a minority of smokers. It has been suggested that there is a hereditary predisposition to lung cancer. If so, it would be helpful to identify the high-risk smoker. Studies have indicated that there is an enzyme present in the pulmonary macrophages and lymphocytes which becomes more active on exposure to cigarette smoke. The wide differences between individuals having this activated enzyme appear to be genetic. One study concluded that it may be possible to identify the high-risk smokers through cellular enzymes. More research will be needed to confirm this possibility.[19]

Oral Cancer

Oral cancer comprises about 2.5 percent of all cancers reported.[20] Studies have shown an association between tobacco usage and death by oral cancer. This association has been demonstrated for all different modes of tobacco usage—cigarette, pipe and cigar smoking and tobacco chewing. The development of recurrent oral cancer has a highly significant correlation with continued smoking.[21]

Other Cancers

Data indicate an association between smoking and mortality from pancreatic cancer. Dose-response relationship has been shown for this cancer. No firm relationship between stomach cancer and cigarette smoking has been established. However a study in Japan extends the association between cigarette smoking and gastric ulcer mortality.[22] Other cancers such as of the esophagus, larynx, pancreas, kidney and urinary bladder are more likely to develop in smokers rather than nonsmokers. These cancers are rare, but it can reasonably be expected that as more studies are completed we will see more links between smoking and other types of cancer.

SMOKING AND CARDIOVASCULAR DISEASE

In the United States, coronary heart disease (CHD) is the leading cause of death and is the largest contributor to deaths among cigarette smokers. Many studies identify cigarette smoking, elevated serum cholesterol and high blood pressure as major factors in the development of CHD. Cigarette smoking acts independently of and synergistically with other factors to increase the risk of developing coronary heart disease. Pipe and cigar smokers have much lower rates of CHD than do cigarette smokers. The increased risk of CHD is greater for younger men, especially those below age 50. Cessation of smoking is associated with decreased risk of death from CHD. Figure 4-7 shows the effects of smoking on cardiovascular functions.

Recent studies have shown that carbon monoxide plays an important part in the way cigarette smoking increases CHD. According to the WHO Expert Committee,

> . . . Carbon monoxide is present in concentration of 1–5% in the gaseous phase of cigarette smoke. The concentration varies with the temperature at which the cigarette burns as well as with factors controlling oxygen supply, such as porosity of the paper. The amount of carbon monoxide produced increases toward the end of the cigarette. Reported carboxyhaemoglobin levels in smokers vary from 2–15% depending on the amount smoked, the degree of inhalation, the time elapsed since the last cigarette was smoked, and the laboratory technique used. Carbon monoxide, which has a much greater affinity for haemoglobin than does oxygen, impairs oxygen transportation in two ways: First it competes with oxygen for haemoglobin binding sites, and second, it increases the affinity of the remaining haemoglobin for oxygen, so that in a given time, a smaller amount of oxygen is released to the tissues.[23]

Other ways cigarette smoking may add to the development of CHD include:

> a. Cigarette smoking, by contributing to the release of catecholamines, causes increased myocardial wall tension, contraction velocity, and heart rate, and thereby increases the work of the heart and the myocardial demand for oxygen and other nutrients.

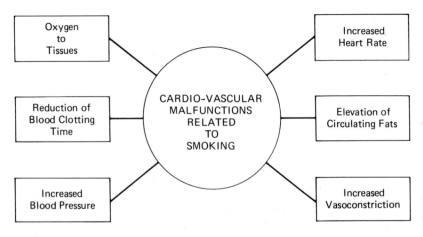

FIG. 4-7 Cardiovascular Diseases and Smoking

b. Among individuals with coronary atherosclerosis, cigarette smoking appears to create an imbalance between the increased needs of the myocardium and an insufficient increase in coronary blood flow and oxygenation.

c. The impairment of pulmonary function caused by cigarette smoking may contribute to arterial hypoxemia, thus reducing the amount of oxygen available to the myocardium.

d. Cigarette smoking may cause an increase in platelet adhesiveness which might contribute to acute thrombus formation.[24]

A study done for the American Cancer Institute by Dr. Hammond resulted in the following conclusions concerning death and coronary heart disease:

1. Death rates from coronary heart disease for men and women 47 to 54 years of age are 2.8 times as high for men and 2 times as high for women who smoke a package or more of cigarettes a day as for nonsmokers.

2. Death rates increase with the number of cigarettes smoked per day, with the degree of inhalation, and with the age at which smoking was begun—it is one-third higher for those who started after 25 years of age.

3. The greatest relative risk of death from heart disease among smokers as compared with nonsmokers is in the age group 40 to 49, with less difference in each succeeding decade.

4. Coronary death rates are little higher for pipe and cigar smokers than for nonsmokers.

5. Death rates decrease with the cessation of smoking.

6. Microscopic examinations of the hearts of persons who are killed or die from diseases other than coronary heart disease show that there are more plaques—that is raised, roughened spots upon which thrombi tend to develop—and much more extensive atherosclerosis in the coronary arteries of smokers than of nonsmokers.[25]

About 125,000 deaths each year from cardiovascular disease are preventable deaths. Many more deaths from heart disease than from lung cancer are attributable to smoking; yet most people know only that smoking is linked to lung cancer and relatively few know of the association with heart disease. The reasons for this are:

1. The association of cigarette smoking with lung cancer was well established before its association with heart disease was recognized.

2. Cigarette smoking is responsible for most deaths from lung cancer, while such factors as high blood pressure, increased amounts of cholesterol in the blood, overweight, and lack of exercise contribute to coronary heart disease.

3. The risk of a heavy smoker dying from lung cancer is approximately twenty times that of a nonsmoker, while the risk of a heavy smoker dying from coronary heart disease is about three times that of a nonsmoker.[26]

SMOKING AND RESPIRATORY DISEASES

Chronic bronchitis accounted for 25,000 deaths in the U.S. in 1969, and the death rate has been rising rapidly since then. *Bronchitis* is an inflammation of the bronchial tubes or air passageways to and within the lungs. *Emphysema* is a lung disease in which the lungs have lost the ability to bring air in and take air out of the lungs. There are over one million cases of these diseases in the United States and it is increasing.[27] As frightening is the rising toll of sickness and disability from these diseases. Figure 4-8 indicates respiratory malfunctions related to smoking, and Figures 4-9 and 4-10 show the damage to lung tissues in emphysema.

Studies in several countries strongly indicate that smoking is the primary cause of these diseases. Symptomatic and asymptomatic smokers have greater lung damage than do nonsmokers. Those that stop smoking have lowered death rates, improved pulmonary function and decrease in prevalence of pulmonary symptoms.

It has been demonstrated that inhalation of cigarette smoke impairs overall pulmonary clearance, ciliary function and alveolar macrophage function.[28] This simply means that the overall effectiveness of an individual's respiratory system has been lowered and the system cannot perform its expected tasks.

Small abnormalities can be detected in smokers who appear to have normal lung function. It has been suggested that the diseases of

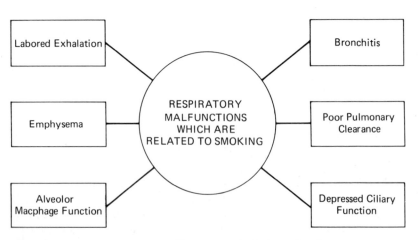

FIG. 4-8   Major Respiratory Malfunctions Which are Related to Smoking

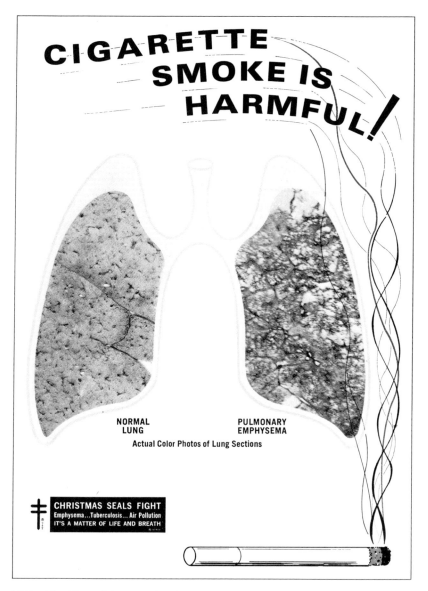

FIG. 4-9 Normal Lung and Pulmonary Emphysema *(Courtesy of the American Lung Association.)*

small airways which cause the abnormalities may later worsen to the point of chronic airway obstruction. Airway obstruction develops slowly over a number of years; if it could be detected by simple tests in middle age, corrective action could be taken before the individual became disabled. Disability usually occurs at over 60 years of age. Cessation of smoking stops accelerated development of obstruction

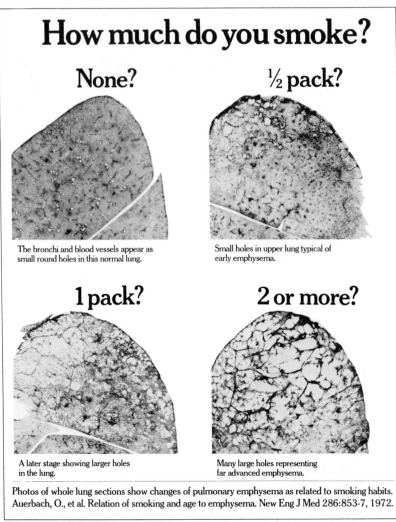

How much do you smoke?

None?

The bronchi and blood vessels appear as small round holes in this normal lung.

½ pack?

Small holes in upper lung typical of early emphysema.

1 pack?

A later stage showing larger holes in the lung.

2 or more?

Many large holes representing far advanced emphysema.

Photos of whole lung sections show changes of pulmonary emphysema as related to smoking habits. Auerbach, O., et al. Relation of smoking and age to emphysema. New Eng J Med 286:853-7, 1972.

FIG. 4-10 How Much do you Smoke? *(Adapted from Chart by the U. S. Public Health Service.)*

seen in smokers. Thus, screening in middle life could be used to detect smokers who will become disabled if they continue to smoke.

SMOKING AND PREGNANCY

Studies in England and Ontario[29] have shown that the lowered birthweight found in babies born to mothers who smoke during pregnancy is a result of a retarded fetal growth rate instead of a shortened gestation period. This is probably due to a high level of carboxyhemoglobin in the fetal blood; it is higher in the fetal blood than in the peripheral blood of the mother tested at the same time.[30]

Cigarette smoking alone is not sufficient to raise the risk of fetal mortality, but when added to other factors the risk is increased, so that mothers who already have a high risk of perinatal mortality should not smoke. In addition, there is some evidence that children of mothers who smoke during pregnancy may be smaller and show slightly lower levels of achievement by age of seven.[31]

THE PSYCHOLOGY OF SMOKING

Despite all the evidence that smoking is damaging to health, people still smoke. Teenage smoking has been on the rise. In 1972 among males 12–18 years old, 15.7 percent smoked, an increase of 1 percent since 1968. In the same four-year period the percent of female teenage smokers increased from 8.4 percent to 13.3 percent. Based on Bureau of Census figures, then, there are 4 million teenagers smoking—an increase of one million over the four-year period.

One of the strongest influences on teenage smokers is the family. If both parents smoke, teenagers are likely to do so also. Increase in likelihood of smoking also exists if an older sibling smokes or if one or both parents are missing from home.

Sociological factors affect a person's decision to smoke. Fewer males and females living on farms smoke than those living in the cities. The higher the income level and the greater the number of years of education, the less likely a person is to smoke. But in regard to the amount smoked, heavy smokers (male) tend to have higher incomes and higher educational attainment. The woman who smokes heavily is likely to be from lower income and lower educational groups.

First Smoke

A national conference on smoking and health revealed that four of five teenagers attempt to smoke.[32] Why? Perhaps because of curiosity, because of the challenge to do so, or to see what the consequences are. Limiting smoking to those age 18 or over simply makes it more desirable. There is an appeal to imitate the behavior of adults, and if it is unlawful or forbidden, the attractiveness of the act actually increases. Whatever the reason for the first smoke Figure 4-11 reveals how many people feel about an individual taking the first smoke.

The initial reaction after the first cigarette is often a negative one. Therefore, it requires choice to be a smoker after the first experimentation. Choosing to smoke requires learning with a positive reinforcement. For the behavior to occur again, the positive reward must follow closely in time and gradually the initial unpleasant consequence take on positive characteristics. Over time, tolerance to nicotine also develops.

Relaxing with a cigarette is a learned experience. As smoking has been paired with a relaxing event, gradually the two behaviors become equated. Some smokers stop because the positive reinforcers are not there. For other people the positive reinforcement is so great so as to support continuation of the habit.

FIG. 4-11 Most Scientists Agree That the First Smoke Is Not Really a Good Idea (*Source: U. S. Department of Health, Education and Welfare.*)

Smoker's Personality Profile

The followers of Freud believe that men for whom the region of the lips had sexual importance from childhood would in adult life have a powerful motive for smoking. Psychoanalysts regard the habit as substitute gratification originally based on deprivation of the maternal breast at weaning. Studies done comparing age of weaning and early oral activities conflict.[33]

Smokers tend to be impulsive, arousal-seeking, danger-loving risk-takers who are belligerent towards authority. Smokers drink more tea, coffee and alcohol and are prone to car accidents, divorce, and changing of jobs.[34]

A study done in England indicates the more a person smokes, the more extroverted is that person. Both pipe smokers and non-smokers were least extroverted.[35]

Several studies indicate that smokers tend to live faster and more intently and to be more socially outgoing. Perhaps extroversion is expressed by smoking, or perhaps because the extrovert participates in these activities he exposes himself to more social stimuli to pick up and reinforce the smoking habit. The smoker may be more sensitive to social influences.[36] Figure 4-12 shows some characteristics of smokers.

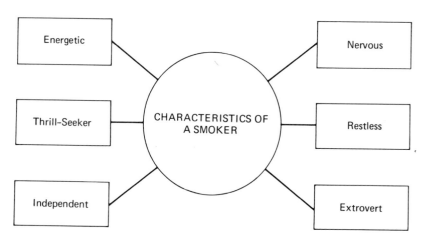

FIG. 4-12   Characteristics of a Smoker

Smoking and Stress

Smoking may be a response to stress and a means of releasing tension. Some studies show that experience of a stressful situation contributes to the beginning of the habit, to its continuation and to the number of cigarettes smoked.[37]

Kissen concludes that "cigarette consumption increases in relation to the occurrence of some emotionally stressful situation. Such situations therefore appear to play a part in perpetuating smoking. The interpretation of what is emotionally stressful may depend on its particular significance to the individual, that is, it may depend on personality traits of the individual."[38]

The same experience of stress in a social situation can provide opportunity for the initial experiments of smoking and can reinforce the habit once it is started.

CESSATION OF SMOKING

There are five social influences affecting the decision to stop smoking (see Figure 4-13):

1. Doctor's attitude, and whether smoker is advised to give up smoking by a physician.
2. The general climate in which the smoker lives. Is it supportive or nonsupportive of smoking?

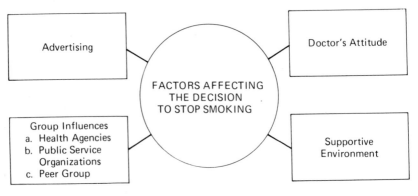

FIG. 4-13　Factors Affecting the Decision to Stop Smoking

3. Advertising influences a smoker. Can the potential quitter ignore it?
4. Key group influences—the kinds of groups whose influences you respect, i.e., health agencies or public service organizations.
5. Interpersonal influences. Are the important people around the smoker supportive of the decision not to smoke?[39]

What are the benefits of quitting? The smoker who gives up smoking will feel better and breathe easier. The risk of developing heart disease or lung cancer is reduced. The longer the person stays away from cigarettes the closer his health condition approaches that of a nonsmoker.

The first three weeks likely will be the hardest. The exsmoker finds it rougher if he had been using smoking as a crutch or tension reducer. Some smokers quit "cold turkey," others over a period of time. A synthetic nicotine substitute lozenge may be used as an aid in stopping. It acts to alter the taste of the cigarette in the mouth. Tranquilizers and sedatives may be necessary for calming during withdrawal.

Hypnotism is used mainly to convince the patient he needs to stop smoking. It can be used to create negative feelings about cigarettes; this technique is an example of aversive deconditioning. This procedure is difficult and there is a lack of valid evaluation to determine effectiveness of the technique.

Reasons for success or failure in stopping smoking are not clear. Smokers motivated by social factors are most likely to succeed. But dependent smokers succeed if they are supported by exsmokers, family or friends. Acceptance of the harmful effect of cigarettes also provides a powerful motive. This is especially true for doctors and men in the higher economic classes.[40] A recent editorial made the following suggestions in terms of needed intervention steps:

1. The promotion of antismoking campaigns;
2. The conduct of carefully designed community-based intervention trials to estimate the impact of cessation of smoking on health states; and
3. The conduct of carefully designed studies, and perhaps reanalysis of existing ones, in order to elucidate accurately the role of environmental and industrial factors. In short, we must not continue evading action in favor of argument. We possess both sufficient empiric grounds and a strong moral obligation to proceed from

where we are, through conscientious intervention programs and creative environmental studies, toward refining our understanding of lung cancer etiology.[41]

SUMMARY

This chapter has dealt with the history of cigarette consumption and its current prevalence; death rates as a result of cigarette smoking; the physical effects of smoking a cigarette; the risks of heart disease, lung cancer and other cancers, bronchitis and emphysema; and a typical smoker's personality.

 It is our conclusion that the risks of smoking are far greater than the benefits. Stop smoking for your own health's sake, and if you haven't started smoking, *don't!* As Figure 4-14 recommends, don't get hooked. A reduction in the number of smokers would result in enormous savings in health and in money for individuals, families and society. There would be fewer work-hours lost and a significant

FIG. 4-14 The Risks of Smoking and the Advantage of Stopping Clearly Tell Us to Not Get Hooked (*Source: U. S. Department of Health, Education and Welfare.*)

reduction in costs to business and industry. In summary, smoking is counterproductive to health and the quality of life in many ways and the reduction and/or cessation of smoking by individuals will enhance health and the quality of life.

BIBLIOGRAPHY (CHAPTER 4)

American Cancer Society, Inc., *The Dangers of Smoking–The Benefits of Quitting*. New York: American Cancer Society, Inc., 1972.

DIEHL, HAROLD S., *Tobacco and Your Health: The Smoking Controversy*. New York: McGraw-Hill, 1969.

DOLL, R., and A. B. HILL, "Mortality in Relation to Smoking: Ten Years Observation of British Doctors," *British Medical Journal* 1 (1964).

GOLD, ROBERT S., WILLIAM H. ZIMMERLI, and WINNIFRED K. AUSTIN, *Comprehensive Bibliography of Existing Literature on Tobacco: 1969 to 1974*. Dubuque, Iowa: Kendall/Hunt Publishing, 1975.

HAMMOND, E.C., "Smoking in Relation to the Death Rates of One Million Men and Women," *National Cancer Institute Monograph* 19 (Jan. 1966).

HAMMOND, E. C., and DANIEL HORN. "Smoking and Death Rates: Report on 44 Months of Follow-up on 187,783 Men," *Journal of American Medical Association* 166 (1958).

Narcotics Education, Inc., *Smoke Signals*, Vol. XVI., Dec. 1970. Mountain View, California: Pacific Press Publishing Association.

National Interagency Council on Smoking and Health, *National Conference on Smoking and Health*. New York: National Interagency Council on Smoking and Health, 1970.

Royal College of Physicians, *Smoking and Health Now*. London: Pitman Medical and Scientific Publishing Co., 1971.

TOZER, ELIOT. *The Thinking Man's Guide to Quitting Cigarettes*. New York: American Cancer Society, 1971.

U.S. Department of Health, Education and Welfare, *The Health Consequences of Smoking*. DHEW Publication No. (CDC) 74-8704, 1974.

U.S. Department of Health, Education and Welfare, *Chart Book on Smoking, Tobacco, and Health*. Washington, D.C., 1973.

World Health Organization, *Smoking and Its Effects on Health*. Report of a WHO Expert Committee, Technical Report Series 568, World Health Organization, Geneva, 1975.

FOOTNOTES (CHAPTER 4)

[1]United States Department of Health, Education and Welfare, *Smoking and Health* (Washington, D.C.: U.S. Government Printing Office, 1964).

[2]Harold S. Diehl, *Tobacco and Your Health: The Smoking Controversy* (New York: McGraw-Hill, 1969), p. 10.

[3]American Cancer Society, Inc., *The Damages of Smoking—The Benefits of Quitting* (New York: American Cancer Society, 1972), p. 7.

[4]Narcotics Education Inc., *Smoke Signals* (Mountain View, California: Pacific Press Publishing Association, 1970), Vol. XVI (Dec.), p. 2.

[5]Diehl, *op. cit.*, p. 51.

[6]U.S. Department of Health, Education, and Welfare, *Chart Book on Smoking, Tobacco, and Health* (Washington, D.C., 1973), pp. 3–4.

[7]R. Doll, and A.B. Hill, "Mortality in Relation to Smoking: Ten Years Observation of British Doctors," *British Medical Journal* 1, (1964), pp. 1399–1460.

[8]E. C. Hammond, "Smoking in Relation to the Death Rates of One Million Men and Women," *National Cancer Institute Monograph* 19, (Jan. 1966), pp. 127–204.

[9]U.S. Surgeon General's Advisory Committee on Smoking and Health, *Smoking and Health Report*, Washington, D.C., U.S. Department of Health, Education and Welfare (Public Health Service Publication No. 1103, 1964), pp. 35–36.

[10]E. C. Hammond and Daniel Horn, "Smoking and Death Rates: Report on 44 Months of Follow-up on 187,783 Men," *Journal of American Medical Association* 166 (1958) pp. 1159–94.

[11]Diehl, *op. cit.*, pp. 27–30.

[12]*Ibid.*

[13]*Ibid.*, p. 34

[14]American Cancer Society, *op. cit.*, p. 21.

[15]U.S. Department of Health, Education and Welfare, *The Health Consequences of Smoking*, DHEW Publication No. HSM 73-8704, 1973, p. 67.

[16]World Health Organization, *Smoking and Its Effects on Health*, Report of a WHO Expert Committee, Technical Report Series 568, (Geneva: World Health Organization, 1975), pp. 9–10.

[17]Royal College of Physicians, *Smoking and Health Now* (London: Pitman Medical and Scientific Publishing Company Ltd., 1971), pp. 24–34.

[18]World Health Organization, *op. cit.*, p. 12.

[19]*Ibid.*, pp. 10–11.

[20]U.S. Department of Health, Education and Welfare, *The Health Consequences of Smoking*, DHEW Publications No. (CDC) 74-8704, 1974, pp. 52–53.

[21]*Ibid.*, pp. 53–54.

[22]*Ibid.*, pp. 56–57.

[23]World Health Organization, *op. cit.*, p. 13.

[24]U.S. Department of Health, Education and Welfare, *The Health Consequences of Smoking: A Report to the Surgeon General* (Washington, D.C.: U.S. Government Printing Office, 1971), pp. 8–9.

[25]Diehl, *op. cit.*, p. 77.

[26]*Ibid.*, pp. 78–79.

[27]National Heart and Lung Institute, *Respiratory Diseases: A Task Force Report on Problems, Research Approaches, Needs*, Washington, D.C.: U.S. Government Printing Office, 1973, pp. 48–49.

[28]U.S. Department of Health, Education and Welfare, *The Health Consequences of Smoking*, pp. 106–107.

[29]World Health Organization, *op. cit.*, p. 15.

[30]*Ibid.*

[31]*Ibid.*

[32]National Interagency Council on Smoking and Health, *National Conference on Smoking and Health* (New York: National Interagency Council on Smoking and Health, 1970), pp. 157–86.

[33]The Royal College of Physicians, *op. cit.*, pp. 110–11.

[34]*Ibid.*, pp. 111–12.

[35]U.S. Department of Health, Education and Welfare, *Smoking and Health*, pp. 365–66.

[36]*Ibid.*, p. 366.

[37]*Ibid.*, p. 373.

[38]*Ibid.*, pp. 373–74.

[39]Eliot Tozer, *The Thinking Man's Guide to Quitting Cigarettes* (New York: American Cancer Society, 1971), pp. 90–91.

[40]*Ibid.*, p. 139.

[41]Michael A. Ibrahim, "The Cigarette Smoking/Lung Cancer Hypothesis," *American Journal of Public Health* 66, No. 2 (Feb. 1976), p. 133.

five

DRUG USE AND ABUSE

Chapters 1 and 2 discussed the social implications of the use and abuse of drugs and the theories of drug dependence; Chapter 3 discussed the use and abuse of the drug, alcohol. We pointed out that each individual must weigh the risks and benefits of drug use, and the potential for abuse. To make this judgment, one must know the kinds of drugs available today, both legal and illegal, and understand how they affect the body and mind.

LEGAL DRUGS

Over-the-counter (OTC) and prescription drugs are a fixture in the American health-care delivery system. These are the "ethical pharmaceuticals." From the middle of the 19th century until the beginning of this century, proprietary (manufactured and sold exclusively by an individual or organization) drugs were ever present and available to consumers. "Snake oil" and other panaceas were thrust upon a gullible public. In the past fifty years, the development of "wonder drugs" such as penicillin and antibiotics have significantly changed the course of disease in man. Most OTC drugs are harmless, if used as directed. However, prescription drugs have a much greater potency and as a result, greater risks are involved.

Prescription Drugs

Prescription drugs are prepared by a pharmaceutical company, prescribed by a licensed physician and dispensed by a registered pharmacist in a hospital or pharmacy. Many of these are truly miracle drugs that have been responsible for reducing pain and suffering, preventing more serious illness and saving many lives. You must rely on the expertise of the physician in prescribing the proper medicine, but you can ask the physician to write the prescription for the generic rather than the brand name. They are the same in therapeutic value, but the generic product might well cost significantly less.

The development of new drugs today is scientifically complex, costly and requires compliance with many governmental regulations. These regulations evolved from the passage of the 1906 Food, Drug and Cosmetic Act. This Act is modified on a continuing basis to keep up with new discoveries.

Pharmaceutical companies are continually searching for new drugs to fight old and newly discovered diseases. They must meet manufacturing requirements determined by the federal agency assigned the task of reviewing, evaluating and approving all new drugs—The Food and Drug Administration. The aim of this process is to produce safe and effective drugs. Frank Clarke, a representative of the pharmaceutical industry, states that:

> The requirements for safety and for demonstrable efficacy make the whole process of introducing a new product long, tedious, demanding and costly. It requires uncommon patience and a dogged capacity to surmount disappointment. But the goal is splendid—nothing short of a safer, more effective agent to alleviate and control disease.[1]

Nonprescription Drugs

There are thousands of nonprescription drugs available on the market today. They are sometimes referred to as *over-the-counter drugs* (OTC) or *proprietary* drugs. If taken as directed, there is little chance that they will have deleterious effects on the consuming public. At the same time, their value must be questioned in many cases.

However, the American Pharmaceutical Association feels that

self medication is an integral part of health care today. People like to medicate themselves—self medication is easy, convenient and generally inexpensive—and it takes some of the load from the already overtaxed physicians.[2]

The individual, of course, takes some risks in using OTC drugs. One must remember that if the symptoms persist, stop any self-medication and seek help from a physician.

The Food and Drug Administration lists the following rules for safe use of nonprescription and prescription drugs:

Don't be casual about taking drugs.
Don't take drugs you don't need.
Don't overbuy and keep drugs for long periods of time.
Don't combine drugs carelessly.
Don't continue taking OTC drugs if symptoms persist.
Don't take prescription drugs not prescribed specifically for you.
Do read and follow directions for use.
Do be cautious when using a drug for the first time.
Do dispose of old prescription drugs and outdated OTC medications.
Do seek professional advice before combining drugs.
Do seek professional advice when symptoms persist or return.
Do get medical check-ups regularly.[3]

Abuse of Conventional Health Products

In the early 1960's a number of Governmental agencies joined together and ordered a study of the health practices and opinions of the American people. This study revealed what many had suspected—that Americans spend millions of dollars annually on products of questionable value. Examples of the conclusions drawn from this study follow:

1. Three-fourths of the public believe that extra vitamins provide more pep and energy, the most common misconceptions investigated. One-fifth agreed that even such diseases as arthritis and cancer are caused, at least in part, by vitamin or mineral deficiencies.
2. Twenty-six percent of the sample, representing about 35 million adults, reported having used nutritional supplements (vitamins and/or minerals, in pills or liquid tonics) expecting actual observable benefits, and without a physician's advice.

3. About 12 percent of the total sample, representing about 16 million adults, reported they had arthritis or rheumatism, asthma, allergies, hemorrhoids, heart trouble, high blood pressure, or diabetes, and that the condition had never been diagnosed by a physician.

4. Twelve percent of the sample, representing about 16 million adults, indicated they would self-medicate, without seeing a doctor, for longer than two weeks for one or more of the following ailments: sore throat, coughs, sinus trouble, head colds, hay fever, skin problems, "helping you sleep", or upset or acid stomach. (Depending upon the ailment, from one-fourth to nearly three-fourths of the sample said they typically do so for more than three days.)

5. Any self-medication for heart trouble, high blood pressure, or diabetes is questionable, as is self-medication of asthma, allergies, or hemorrhoids when a cure, rather than symptomatic relief, is expected. Seven percent of the total sample, representing about nine million adults, was classifed in one or another of these categories.

6. One-fourth of the sample claimed to have arthritis, rheumatism, or some similar disease. About one-fifth of these, however, representing about seven million adults, had not had the condition diagnosed by a physician. Nearly one-fifth of all the "sufferers" had not received treatment from a physician. [4]

Therefore, many Americans do, in fact, indulge in self-diagnosis and self-medication. The study concluded that rampant empiricism seemed to govern the behavior of the consumers. This means that anything is worth a try, and logic and reason are discarded. As a result, money is wasted and often precious time is lost in obtaining conventional health care. This makes recovery, if possible, much more difficult.

ILLEGAL DRUGS

Americans have become increasingly concerned with the abuse of illegal drugs such as heroin, marijuana, stimulant and depressant drugs, and hallucinogens. The awareness of the drug phenomenon seemed to begin around the middle of the 1960's when drug abuse was taking place on college campuses around the nation. Since that time numerous surveys have been undertaken in an effort to determine the number of individuals involved in some type of drug abuse. These surveys are only estimates and cannot be considered absolute answers to the intensity of the drug problem.

The Bureau of Narcotics and Dangerous Drugs has compiled statistics from state and local agencies in an effort to estimate the degree of drug abuse today and to provide indications of the problem in the future. For the years 1969–70, as compared to 1960, there was a 51 percent increase in the number of active addicts and the number of addicts under 21 years of age increased by 173 percent.[5]

A drug abuse summary issued by the National Institute of Mental Health for 1969–70 estimated that there were approximately 100,000 to 200,000 narcotic addicts, with an additional 500,000 dependent upon nonnarcotic drugs.[6] The numbers have increased since this study.

Although earlier studies indicated that a majority of abused drugs were purchased through illegal channels, the new trend appears to be purchased through legal prescriptions.

This marked increase in drug abuse is startling today, but indications for the future may be worse. With modern science continually producing more efficient drugs, increased drug abuse will likely follow.

Most literature focuses on teenage and young adult abusers. Although these groups comprise a large amount of drug abusers, the problem is not confined to just these individuals. Persons from any age group can become involved with drugs. As one individual has suggested,

> We have drugs of the fathers such as coffee, tobacco, alcohol, tranquilizers and barbiturates, and we have drugs of the sons such as marijuana, opiates, stimulants and hallucinogens. Drugs of the fathers make you a little more human. Drugs of the sons make you a little more than human.[7]

Finally, a report to the Ford Foundation rather succinctly summarizes a rational approach toward illegal drugs.

> It is of fundamental importance that man has and will inevitably continue to have potentially dangerous drugs at his disposal, which he may either use properly or abuse, and that neither the availability of these drugs nor the temptation to abuse them can be eliminated. Therefore, the fundamental objective of a modern drug-abuse program must be to help the public learn to understand these drugs and how to cope with their use in the context of everyday life. An approach emphasizing suppression of all drugs or repression of all drug users will only contribute to national problems.[8]

CLASSIFICATION OF DRUGS

Drugs can be and have been classified in many ways; we will use the simplest approach. There are two broad types: legal drugs and illegal drugs. The illegal (street) drugs are costly and are dangerous because they have poor integrity—that is, the quality and reliability are highly variable and even their validity is questionable. The legal drugs, those available either over-the-counter or by prescription, are perhaps the most abused today even though the greatest visibility and concern are given to the street drugs.

Many drugs are capable of being abused if they are used beyond their initial, intended purpose. We shall focus on those drugs most commonly abused. These can be classified into groups according to their effects upon the user.

One group of abused drugs is the *narcotics*. Because the sale of narcotic drugs is illegal in the United States, these dangerous drugs are available strictly through illicit and black-market purchases. The cost of narcotic addiction, as indicated earlier in this book, is very high and has contributed to the increasing number of drug-related crimes. The addict will generally resort to crime to secure money for the drug.

The *barbiturates* or *sedative drugs* have important medical uses and are prescribed by many physicians. In addition, these drugs are purchased illegally by some individuals for the express purpose of abuse. The pusher selling sedatives on the street will more than likely have secured the drugs unlawfully from a pharmacy or physician's office or through forged prescriptions.

Other commonly abused drugs are the *stimulants*. Like sedatives, these drugs are used by physicians in the treatment of various medical problems. These drugs are normally obtained through medical prescriptions although they are purchased and sometimes produced through black-market channels for purposes of abuse. As in the case of sedatives, the peddler or abuser will obtain the drug either by stealing from a pharmacy or doctor or by using forged or stolen prescriptions.

Hallucinogens are another group of abused drugs. Like narcotics, these drugs have no known medical value and the sale and possession of these drugs are illegal in the United States. The hallucinogens are often produced in basement laboratories and are purchased entirely through illegal channels. Table 5-1 provides a brief summary of the most prevalent drugs, their uses and effects.

Stimulants

Stimulants are drugs which speed up the action of the central nervous system. In doing so, the stimulants create a feeling of wakefulness and alertness and create a sense of well-being and self-confidence. They are used to combat fatigue, curb appetite, and reduce mild depression. The most common stimulants are amphetamines, cocaine, coffee, tea, and nicotine.

Amphetamines. Amphetamines are synthetic compounds that have a unique similarity to adrenalin; the amphetamines imitate our own natural reactions to stress and emergency situations by causing an arousal or activating response. Amphetamines are known to decrease appetite and thus are used for weight reduction. Benzedrine and Dexedrine are used for this purpose and are among the most frequently abused amphetamines. These *pep pills*, as they are known to abusers, not only reduce appetite, but make the individual more active and combat fatigue. Another widely abused amphetamine is Methedrine, commonly referred to as *speed.*

Large doses of amphetamines cause over-stimulation; the user becomes nervous, jittery and oversensitive to stimuli. Large doses used frequently are psychologically habit forming. Because amphetamines suppress symptoms of fatigue, an individual is apt to continue beyond his physical endurance. Thus, when effects of the drugs wear off, extreme feelings of exhaustion and depression result. This is referred to as a "crash," one of the characteristics of these drugs. In an effort to escape effects of this crash, the user will depend on more pills and a cycle of dependence will result. Tolerance to amphetamines increases rapidly, with higher doses necessary to obtain the original effects.

Amphetamines are generally consumed in tablet form although they can be sniffed as crystal or injected to obtain faster effects.

The major medical uses for amphetamines are in the treatment of narcolepsy and hyperactivity and for weight reduction.

Cocaine. Cocaine is a stimulating substance derived from the leaves of the coca bush. Legally, cocaine is classified as a narcotic even though it is stimulating in effect.

Cocaine is a white, crystalline powder which can be sniffed,

Table 5-1. Controlled Substances: Uses and Effects

	DRUGS	SCHEDULE	OFTEN PRESCRIBED BRAND NAMES	MEDICAL USES	DEPENDENCE PHYSICAL
NARCOTICS	Opium	II	Dover's Powder, Paregoric	Analgesic, antidiarrheal	High
	Morphine	II	Morphine	Analgesic	High
	Codeine	II, III, V	Codeine	Analgesic, antitussive	Moderate
	Heroin	I	None	None	High
	Meperidine (Pethidine)	II	Demerol, Pethadol	Analgesic	High
	Methadone	II	Dolophine, Methadone, Methadose	Analgesic, heroin substitute	High
	Other Narcotics	I, II, III, V	Dilaudid, Leritine, Numorphan, Percodan	Analgesic, antidiarrheal, antitussive	High
DEPRESSANTS	Chloral Hydrate	IV	Noctec, Somnos	Hypnotic	Moderate
	Barbiturates	II, III, IV	Amytal, Butisol, Nembutal, Phenobarbital, Seconal, Tuinal	Anesthetic, anti-convulsant, sedation, sleep	High
	Glutethimide	III	Doriden	Sedation, sleep	High
	Methaqualone	II	Optimil, Parest, Quaalude, Somnafac, Sopor	Sedation, sleep	High
	Meprobamate	IV	Equanil, Meprospan, Miltown Kesso-Bamate, SK-Bamate	Anti-anxiety, muscle relaxant, sedation	Moderate
	Other Depressants	III, IV	Dormate, Noludar, Placidyl, Valmid	Anti-anxiety, sedation, sleep	Possible
STIMULANTS	Cocaine	II	Cocaine	Local anesthetic	Possible
	Amphetamines	II, III	Benzedrine, Biphetamine, Desoxyn, Dexedrine	Hyperkinesis, narcolepsy, weight control	Possible
	Phenmetrozine	II	Preludin	Weight control	Possible
	Methylphenidate	II	Ritalin	Hyperkinesis,	Possible
	Other Stimulants	III, IV	Bacarate, Cylert, Didrex, Ionamin, Plegine, Pondimin, Pre-Sate, Sanorex, Voranil	Weight control	Possible
HALLUCINOGENS	LSD	I	None	None	None
	Mescaline	I	None	None	None
	Psilocybin-Psilocyn	I	None	None	None
	MDA	I	None	None	None
	PCP	III	Sernylan	Veterinary anesthetic	None
	Other Hallucinogens	I	None	None	None
CANNABIS	Marihuana Hashish Hashish Oil	I	None	None	Degree unknown

Table 5-1. (Cont'd.)

POTENTIAL: PSYCHOLOGICAL	TOLERANCE	DURATION OF EFFECTS (in hours)	USUAL METHODS OF ADMINISTRATION	POSSIBLE EFFECTS	EFFECTS OF OVERDOSE	WITHDRAWAL SYNDROME
High	Yes	3 to 6	Oral, smoked			
High	Yes	3 to 6	Injected, smoked			Watery eyes, runny nose, yawning, loss of appetite, irritability, tremors, panic, chills and sweating, cramps, nausea
Moderate	Yes	3 to 6	Oral, injected	Euphoria drowsiness, respiratory depression, constricted pupils, nausea	Slow and shallow breathing, clammy skin, convulsions, coma, possible death	
High	Yes	3 to 6	Injected, sniffed			
High	Yes	3 to 6	Oral, injected			
High	Yes	12 to 24	Oral, injected			
High	Yes	3 to 6	Oral, injected			
Moderate	Probable	5 to 8	Oral			
High	Yes	1 to 16	Oral, injected			
High	Yes	4 to 8	Oral	Slurred speech, disorientation, drunken behavior without odor of alcohol	Shallow respiration, cold and clammy skin, dilated pupils, weak and rapid pulse, coma, possible death	Anxiety, insomnia, tremors, delirium, convulsions, possible death
High	Yes	4 to 8	Oral			
Moderate	Yes	4 to 8	Oral			
Possible	Yes	4 to 8	Oral			
High	Yes	2	Injected, sniffed			
High	Yes	2 to 4	Oral, injected	Increased alertness, excitation, euphoria, dilated pupils, increased pulse rate and blood pressure insomnia, loss of appetite.	Agitation, increase in body temperature, hallucinations, convulsions, possible death.	Apathy, long period of sleep, irritability, depression, disorientation.
High	Yes	2 to 4	Oral			
High	Yes	2 to 4	Oral			
Possible	Yes	2 to 4	Oral			
Degree unknown	Yes	Variable	Oral			
Degree unknown	Yes	Variable	Oral, injected			
Degree unknown	Yes	Variable	Oral	Illusions and hallucinations (with exception of MDA); poor perception of time and distance	Longer, more intense "trip" episodes, psychosis, possible death	Withdrawal syndrome not reported
Degree unknown	Yes	Variable	Oral, injected, sniffed			
Degree unknown	Yes	Variable	Oral, injected, smoked			
Degree unknown	Yes	Variable	Oral, injected, sniffed			
Moderate	Yes	2 to 4	Oral, smoked	Euphoria, relaxed inhibitions, increased appetite, disoriented behavior	Fatigue, paranoia, possible psychosis	Insomnia, hyperactivity, and decreased appetite reported a limited number individuals

SOURCE: Drug Enforcement, Drug Enforcement Administration, U.S. Department of Justice, Spring, 1975

swallowed or injected in liquid form; it is not physically addicting as there are no withdrawal symptoms when use is stopped. However, tolerance and psychological dependence do develop in the same manner as with amphetamines. Cocaine produces similar feelings of euphoria and mood elevation as amphetamines, but these feelings last for a shorter length of time and are followed by depression which is relieved by taking another dose.[9] The unusually grand feelings of euphoria probably account for abuse of this drug.

Coffee and Tea. These stimulants are socially accepted and are not toxic unless used in very large doses. They have stimulating effects upon the individual but tend to be milder than amphetamines and cocaine.

Depressants

Depressants, or sedatives, are drugs that slow down the action of the central nervous system. These drugs act to reduce tension and anxiety, and induce sleep. The most commonly abused depressants are barbiturates.[10] Alcohol and tranquilizers also belong to this group of drugs.

Barbiturates. Barbiturates are generally prescribed as sleeping pills, and when used as directed by a physician, produce very few side effects. When these drugs are abused and consumed in large doses, they become very dangerous and are physically addictive when used without control. These drugs have an intoxicating effect and lead to extreme mental and emotional confusion with painful withdrawal symptoms when use is stopped. Death can and often does result from an overdose of these drugs or from abrupt withdrawal.

The most commonly abused barbiturates are Seconal, Nembutal, (phenobarbital), Tuinal and Amytal. All of these are consumed in capsule form and abusers refer to them by their colors—i.e., reds or redbirds for Seconal, yellows or yellow jackets for Amytal.

These drugs are used medically for treatment requiring sedation or a hypnotic state to reduce anxiety, for example, in psychiatric and post-surgical situations.

The barbiturates are extremely dangerous drugs and are a

leading cause of death by poison, either by suicide or by accidental overdose. These drugs become very lethal when combined with alcohol due to the additive depressant effects upon the body.

Narcotics

The term *narcotic* generally refers to opium and pain-killing drugs derived from opium, such as heroin, morphine, paregoric and codeine. The opiates are obtained from juices of the poppy fruit. Heroin is by far the most popular of the opiates used by addicts.

The main effect of narcotics are to deaden feelings and relieve pain, to induce sleep and to give a sense of well-being. These drugs essentially depress action of the central nervous system. The intensity of the euphoric feeling is the probable reason for abuse. The body develops a tolerance to narcotics, requiring increased amounts of the drug to overcome withdrawal effects. Narcotics are true addicting drugs with physical addiction occurring quickly. The narcotic abuser tends to be in a stuporous dreamy state while under effects of the drug.

Narcotics can be administered orally in pill, capsule, or powder form, or injected under the skin, into a muscle, or directly into a vein for faster action.

Opium. Opium is a natural substance derived from the dried juice of the oriental poppy. In the raw form, it is smoked in a pipe or eaten to obtain desired effects. In the United States it is rarely used in this raw form, but rather its derivatives are used.

Morphine. Morphine is the primary derivative of opium, making it a natural narcotic. It is one of the most effective means of pain relief in use today and is quickly addicting. Morphine can be found in various forms such as crystals, powder, pills, or capsules. It can be swallowed, but is generally injected under the skin or into a vein. Morphine has much stronger effects than opium and is used in hospital settings. Very little morphine is peddled on the streets.

Heroin. Heroin is a semisynthetic substance produced from morphine. It is 20–25 times stronger in effect and has twice the addictive power, thus making it a very dangerous drug.[11]

Heroin is generally a white to light-brown powder that is

sniffed or injected under the skin or into a vein. Most of the heroin entering this country now comes from Mexico. It is the most expensive form of addiction. It is sold by the ounce or in smaller packages on the streets. The market for heroin is strictly illegal and there are no medical uses whatsoever.

Heroin is considered an extremely dangerous drug and physical addiction is greater than with other narcotics due to the rapid development of tolerance. Heroin addicts become dangerous when they do not get their heroin, but otherwise are not a threat. The intense euphoric experience obtained with heroin accounts for its popularity in the drug world. Very painful withdrawal symptoms occur when the drug is not administered regularly. Complaints and demands by the addict peak about 36 to 72 hours after the last dose. Other symptoms (see controlled substance chart) appear about 8 to 12 hours after the last dose. Most of the symptoms, without treatment, will disappear in about 7 to 10 days. However, return to complete physiological and psychological balance is unpredictable. The heroin cycle involves continued use to counteract the sickness of withdrawal, thus making complete cure from addiction very difficult.

Methadone. Methadone is a synthetic narcotic drug which has been used in some treatment and rehabilitation programs. It is, chemically, different than heroin, but it produces many of the same effects. There are a number of medically supervised methadone programs in the United States. However, physical dependence and tolerance can develop and withdrawal symptoms occur that are similar to those of heroin users—only at a slower rate.

The medically supervised methadone treatment regimen has been widely used since the 1960's in detoxification of heroin addicts and in methadone maintenance programs. The advantages of this program include: (1) letting the individual lead a more normal life, (2) attenuated withdrawal symptoms, (3) free treatment, and (4) a likelihood that the individual will cooperate in the rehabilitation process.

Codeine. Codeine is a natural derivative of opium that is milder in effect than morphine and heroin.[12] Codeine is not widely abused as it must be consumed in rather large amounts to achieve the desired euphoric effects. Narcotic addicts may use codeine when they cannot obtain a supply of heroin, even though the overall effects are much milder.

Codeine is important medically because it suppresses coughing. Therefore, it is used widely in cough formulas. Because codeine is a narcotic and addiction can occur, restricted amounts are found in over-the-counter formulas sold in the United States.

Hallucinogens

Hallucinogens, or psychedelic drugs, are those with capabilities to create vivid sensual distortions without totally disturbing a user's consciousness. This drug group is comprised of naturally occurring and synthetic drugs. Hallucinogens have no valid therapeutic value as yet, although research is being conducted for possible use with mentally ill patients. The most commonly abused hallucinogens are LSD, marijuana and mescaline.

The overall effects of these drugs are to alter mood and perception. When taken in small doses, they are euphoriant in nature and the user's consciousness is not affected. When larger doses are consumed, reactions can range from horror to ecstasy, with a possibility of hallucinations resulting.[13]

LSD. The man-made chemical, lysergic acid diethylamide, is a very powerful mind-affecting drug. This drug is a threat because it is so easily manufactured. The average dose of LSD is very minute, yet it is capable of producing extreme reactions. The drug acts on the mind, causing varied psychic experiences. Sensory perception is especially affected; one may see objects change shape and dimensions. Color and depth perceptions are increased and an individual can lose touch with the environment while under the effects of the drug. Bad as well as good psychic experiences occur, depending on the user's psychological condition at the time the drug is used.

Some rather bizarre experiences may occur, making LSD a dangerous drug. Panic and paranoia may develop as users become frightened and suspicious of the drug's effects. Recurrence of effects ("flash backs") can take place up to months after initial use and some accidental deaths have occurred when a user feels he can fly or cannot be harmed while under these effects.[14]

LSD is not physically addicting, but one can become psychologically dependent upon its use. It is usually eaten after it has been placed on objects such as sugar cubes or cookies, or it is licked from the back of stamps.

Marijuana. Marijuana is one of the many terms used for the various intoxicating preparations produced from the Indian hemp plant, *Cannabis sativa*. Other more powerful preparations include hashish and hashish oil. Some of the many slang terms used for marijuana are pot, joints, charge, tea, grass and Acapulco gold. It is considered to be the least powerful hallucinogenic drug, and is usually smoked in cigarette form.

The principal psychoactive substance in marijuana is thought to be delta-9-tetrahydrocannabinol (THC). Users may experience a feeling of euphoria, restlessness, an alteration of sensory perceptions and a more acute sense of touch, sight, smell, taste and sound. Higher doses may result in distortions of body image, loss of personal identity, fantasies and hallucinations.[15]

A number of research studies on the effects of marijuana have been conducted in recent years, and the conclusions have varied. *Consumer Reports* feels that:

Out of all of these many studies . . . a general pattern is beginning to emerge. When a research finding can be readily checked—either by repeating the experiment or by devising a better one—an allegation of adverse marijuana effects is relatively short-lived. No damage is found—and after a time the allegation is dropped (often to be replaced by allegations of some other kind of damage due to marijuana).[16]

On the other hand, the Drug Enforcement Administration has stated:

Despite preliminary reports to the contrary, there have been several papers in scientific journals since 1971 that document the dependence-producing properties of cannabis.[17]

A Federal Strategy Council on Drug Abuse concluded that:

The central issue is whether in light of these estimates and the effect of the drug, current attempts to prohibit the availability and use of cannabis products should be abandoned or modified.

We do not believe that a change in policy is warranted at this time. The control of marijuana abuse will continue to be a Federal drug control objective for the following reasons:

New, more potent forms of cannabis derivatives are becoming available. A very disturbing development in the illicit traffic is the increasing appearance of hashish oil—a liquid concentrate of THC, the psychoactive ingredient of marijuana. The potency of this substance is many times greater than that of marijuana or even ordinary hashish. The possible adverse long-term effects of this powerful hallucinogen may be significant, but are not yet fully understood.

The effects of chronic heavy use of cannabis and the effects of regular marijuana use have yet to be fully determined. An extended period of time elapsed between the widespread use of tobacco and the demonstration of its deleterious effects. Much marijuana research has been inconclusive, but occasional adverse findings such as tissue damage to the throat and trachea continue to appear.

The nation's experience with alcohol and tobacco suggests that once consumption of a drug becomes woven into the fabric of society through custom and ritual, subsequent elimination is virtually impossible. Thus, decisions which increase the extent of use are generally irreversible.

We are aware of the assertions that few individuals are deterred from marijuana use by the present legal prohibitions and that only a small percentage of total arrests result in imprisonment. Nonetheless the extent of use would probably be far greater in the absence of such continued sanctions. We are not in favor of any measures which would tend to increase the total number of users and, hence, the potential number of heavy users.[18]

The controversial issue being discussed, written about and debated is, of course, whether the use of marijuana should be legalized. Sidney Cohen, in his book *The Drug Dilemma*, has described the predictable developments if marijuana is legalized in similar fashion to alcohol.

1. The number of users will increase. Surveys indicate that about 10 percent of students and larger numbers of older adults do not smoke because it is illegal. On the other hand, those who smoke predominantly as a protest against the Establishment may stop.

2. As total numbers increase, the number of heavy users will increase.

3. The strength of the cannabis used will increase. This trend is already noticeable, with more hashish being consumed now than in the past. No doubt, one day, pure THC will become available outside the research laboratory. Legalization would probably not include the stronger cannabis preparations.

4. It will still be illegal to sell to minors, but they will become involved in greater numbers than at present.

5. The consumption of alcoholic beverages will not decrease. At one time the substitution of marijuana for alcohol was put forth as an argument for legalization. More recently it has become clear that marijuana users also consume their share of alcoholic beverages.

6. The smoking of tobacco products will be relatively unaffected. There have been no signs of a shift away from tobacco by cannabis users.

7. Increased federal and state revenues will accrue. About a billion dollars a year in taxes and fees would result from regulating marijuana. Less than 10,000 acres would grow the amount needed to supply domestic requirements.[19]

Controversy has raged over the existing laws on the use of marijuana. There has been a movement to legalize its use, or at least to decriminalize its possession in small amounts. The advantages and disadvantages of marijuana use will have to be discussed, evaluated and decided upon by the American people. Their decision will serve as a mandate to the lawmakers, one way or the other.

CHARACTERISTICS OF DRUG ABUSERS

It is difficult, if not impossible, to draw a definitive profile of a drug user that is applicable to all drug users. This is true, of course, because people are different in so many ways—in life-style, goals, motivation, environmental factors and individual problems.

Although drug abusers do not have any age limitations, it may be helpful to take a close look at young abusers. Young adulthood is a time that can be compared to a butterfly when it is first coming out of its cocoon. There has been protection from life, but the time for change and exploration has arrived and one must try one's wings. There is a degree of idealism at this stage which is at the highest level of any period of a life.

The need for experimentation at this age has not changed for many generations; only the choice of drugs has changed. The drugs in previous generations were alcohol and tobacco. Parents cannot be as objective about marijuana as their parents were about alcohol and tobacco because they lack knowledge of the drug, and fear that this will only be the beginning of a pattern which will lead to complete drug dependence.

The high school and college years are usually thought of as the important transition period between childhood and adulthood. Many of life's vital decisions are made during these years—the type and amount of further education, career choice, marriage and place of residence.

Young people are bombarded from all angles—television, radio, newspapers, magazines—with the propaganda of an improved life through chemistry. Peer group influence is dominant to that of parents. With such a deluge of information, there is little surprise that the young adult finds it difficult to sort out the facts and make the right decision in terms of positive health status.

There are eight categories of values which are universal to mankind. These provide us with a method of access to the process of attitude formation and modification. They are: (1) affection, (2) respect, (3) well-being, (4) enlightenment, (5) rectitude, (6) power, (7) skill and (8) wealth. The choice which a person will make is largely determined by his self-concept as based on these categories.[20] The final decision, of course, must be made by the individual. There will be many outside influences, but the individual alone must decide what to do. Part of this decision will be determined on the basis of the relationship of the perceived rewards and costs.

Drug abusers can be divided into three categories: the experience seeker, the oblivion seeker and the personality-change seeker.[21]

The *experience seeker* is an individual who is motivated by the social pressures to experiment or by the fascination of the dangers of addiction, arrest or death. Many times the motive is to shock one's parents into having some awareness of personal needs. If this is not effective, the individual may have to rely on another adult in the community to fill the void.

The *oblivion seeker* finds that a drugged state is a wonderful release from the pressures of the world. His involvement with drugs is more chronic. These people are frequently the drop-outs from society who have been rejected by both parents and society. This type of abuser must have his strengths emphasized instead of the weaknesses, and interests in other things need to be stimulated. The self-fulfilling prophecy of failure must be reversed for this person. Help will be needed with the area of conflict. This is not an overnight solution, but the problems did not arise overnight.

The *personality-change seeker* looks for an improvement in personality with the use of drugs, and is disappointed to find that this has not been accomplished. This individual constantly changes drugs and increases dosage in an attempt to find the desired personality. The drugs did not cause this individual's problems, because the basic personality abnormality was there before the first drug was used. The prognosis is poor even when there is prolonged psychiatric care.

Students today learn little in their formal schooling about fundamental issues of adolescence. They must fall back on their own resources in order to determine the real issues. The length of schooling is longer than it was in the past, so young people are kept in a dependent state for a longer time. However, they are judged by adult standards and are expected to demonstrate maturity. Adults appear to be amazed that there could be an identity crisis. However, verbalizing the fact there is an identity crisis is sometimes considered to be a badge of courage, or a scalp at the belt, for the young person.

The goal of immediate need satisfaction has been made a primary one. The experience of the present is stressed over the tradition of the past. The meaning of life must be sought with the present experience of one's self, the activities, and the responsiveness of the here and now.

It seems that there are many different motives for drug abuse, and there are many different factors—psychological, sociological, cultural, and situational—which will determine why one person will use drugs and another will not. The person who seems to be the most prone to drug abuse is the disaffiliate. One characteristic of this person is his generalized rejection of present American values on the grounds of aesthetics, culture and humanism. The disaffiliate is rarely concerned with political, social, or economic issues, but only wants an escape from the stagnation which he feels, signifies our American society.

Another characteristic is an intense feeling of estrangement from one's own experience. This is often accompanied by depression and a strong feeling of isolation. The loss of an important relationship is commonly found in the immediate background of the person who begins to abuse drugs. Drugs that promise to heighten experience appear to be a tempting way out of one's shell.

U.S. STUDIES

A review of the literature in the United States reveals some additional characteristics of drug abusers. To illustrate this point, a study in Alabama was conducted on two groups of males—ten in each group—to determine if there were significant differences between the personality of the multiple abuser and the nonuser, and to characterize these differences, if they did exist. The first group consisted of habitual and gross multiple drug users of the nonnarcotic type. The other group consisted of nonusers.

White males between the ages of 18 and 25 were chosen who had similar educational levels and socioeconomic background, and were of average or above-average intelligence. The Minnesota Multiphasic Personality Inventory was used to assess personality characteristics. The 16PF, a factor analytical personality device, was used to give a comprehensive and objective description of personality structure.

The control group consisted of young men from a junior college. Their manner of dress and hair style were conservative. Their life style appeared to be goal-oriented with a desire for social acceptance and the pursuit of a vocation.

The experimental group was composed of vocational rehabilitation clients who were in this program because of their regular use of drugs. Their manner of dress and hair style were those of nonconformists who had rejected the establishment. Their goals were unrealistic and they made no serious effort to reach these goals. Their only concern was for the present.

The control group tested out as a moderate, stable, almost stereotyped middle class on the PF, while the experimental group showed a marked variability in personality expression.

The researcher concluded that there were gross personality differences between the users and the nonusers. One unanswered question is whether these differences existed before the drug problem began, or were caused by the drugs?[22]

Another U.S. study tried to determine what psychological or sociological factors distinguish marijuana users from nonusers, and the occasional user from the regular user. The study was undertaken with 264 members of a senior high-school class, from a public high school whose students came from middle and upper-middle class families. Approximately eighty-five percent of the students planned to attend college.

Twenty-one percent of the total sample group had abused some type of drug at one time or another. Twenty percent had used marijuana at least one time. There was no significant difference in the academic performance of the regular marijuana users, the occasional users, and nonusers. The drug users showed significantly less devoutness to religion, and more atheism. The nonusers felt that their mothers were more permissive and fathers more strict. The nonusers felt that their parents were fair, but firm. The use of alcohol by the parents of users was highly prevalent. Treatment for emotional problems was much more prevalent in users than nonusers. They were much more likely to have broken the law, to have had trouble in school and to have had sexual experiences. The investigators felt that this study was especially revealing since an entire senior class was studied, and not just drug users.[23]

Studies in Other Countries

The drug user and drug abuser are not unique to the United States. It may be useful and helpful, and may give additional insights, to review some studies that have been done in other countries. A study in London, Ontario, between June and November of 1970, included 98 persons in a treatment network that blended the services of hospitals and clinics. A self-help project was established which utilized both the ex-addict and the professional. Their work was considered therapeutic. The main thrust of the treatment regimen was a reality-oriented peer-controlled encounter group. One finding which was consistent with earlier studies was the high rate of drug use among those who stated that they had no religious affiliation. The self-help project in Ontario recognized that the person enrolled in this program was educationally unprepared to secure a good job, so his educational and vocational skills were upgraded at the same time that his personality and behavior were changed.[24]

In Spain, ninety-five drug user cases were investigated from January 1 to May 1, 1971; all of the subjects were under the age of thirty-one, and none were heroin addicts. The law of Spain provides for the administration of therapeutic doses of narcotic drugs during the detoxification treatment, so these people were in a separate classification. There are few heroin addicts in Spain due to the extremely high cost of the drug.

There were two times as many men as women in the sample. Eighty-six percent of the subjects began to use drugs before the age of twenty. One-half of the sample, regardless of age or sex, had no concrete aspirations in life; this has often been found in other studies.

The average number of children per family in Spain was 2.8; the subjects came from families with an average of 3.2 children. Sixty-eight percent came from homes in which the relationship of the mother and father was regarded to be good. Eighteen percent came from broken homes. The attitude of the parents toward their children was primarily one of tolerance.

The type of friendships preferred did appear to have a close relationship to drug use. The friends that the subjects preferred used drugs, and the majority of the sample were first introduced to drugs by these friends, who appeared to exert a major influence over them.

The subjects displayed a certain consistency in their attitudes toward their family and society which bordered on antagonism and some rejection. It seemed as if they were attempting to escape from reality for a limited time in an atmosphere of less responsible and somewhat marginal friendship. At the same time, they did not want to sever themselves from their family or society.

The author concluded that use of drugs among this group appeared to be due to a desire to satisfy a need—for example, to satisfy curiosity, to escape from routine or to find companionship. He felt that another study was needed to learn why drug users need to satisfy specific appetites, and why they seek these drugs even though they know they are inviting legal and social condemnation.[25]

A Danish hospital-based study was made utilizing a social-psychiatric method. Home visits were made to one hundred and eighty-seven of the three hundred and fifty homes of the subjects who were admitted. It was found that the social and psychiatric factors which were different between the normal and the addicted subjects were the number of broken homes, the number of fathers who were more than forty years old at the time of the child's birth, father's misuse of alcohol and mother's use of psychoactive medicines. Factors which were the same in addict and nonaddict groups were the standards of housing, rural-to-urban moves, un-married mothers, father's psychiatric admissions, father's use of psychoactive medicines, and mother's misuse of alcohol.

It was found that a very large number of the addict's parents had sought assistance from public agencies before the abuse began, and that a high percentage of the parents admitted that there were problems with their child. This was especially true in the lower social class. There was no significant relationship between the psychiatric admission of the parents and children.

The employment picture of these patients is the same as in other countries—extremely high unemployment. Hard drug abuse and lower social class were closely correlated.

When the parents were asked what society could do to help the abusers, the majority stated that they didn't know. Most of them felt that involuntary hospitalization was necessary, but few were satisfied with the care their children received.

Most of the parents felt that the drug usage was the fault of the peer group, sometimes due to the pressure they applied, or to the fact that they had pills slipped into their beer. The parents were well-informed about the behavior of their children with the exception of this misuse of drugs.[26]

The preceding review of studies around the world tends to underscore the similarity of drug users in the world today. That is, drug users tend to be nonconformists, nonreligious, to come from poor home environments, to have no concrete goals for life and, in general, to reject the establishment. The nonusers, on the other hand, tend to have just the opposite characteristics.

SUMMARY

No class of society is immune to drug-taking. Young people are attracting the most attention and eliciting the deepest concern; in many cases these youth have found in drugs a way of rebelling and rejecting family and society. Drug abuse affects the individual involved and society. In recent years drug abuse has become one of the major public health problems in the United States.

Laws to regulate and control drug use have been enacted on both federal and state levels. Rehabilitation services have been developed to help individuals dependent upon drugs.

Thus far, these methods have not eliminated drug abuse. This problem has been with us for generations and will probably remain, but it must be minimized. Society can help control illegal sale and distribution of drugs by educating the public fully about dangers of drug abuse and by strictly enforcing existing laws.

BIBLIOGRAPHY (CHAPTER 5)

BARNES, DONALD E. and LOUISA MESSOLONGHITES, *Preventing Drug Abuse*. Boston: Holt, Rinehart and Winston, 1972.

BASELGA, EDUARDO, "Young Drug Users: Sociological Study of One Sample," *Bulletin on Narcotics* 24 (July-Sept. 1972): 17–22.

BERGEL, FRANZ, and D. R. A. DAVIES, *All About Drugs*. New York: Barnes and Noble, 1972.

BLUMENFIELD, MICHAEL, ALBERT E. REISTER, ALBERTO SERRANO, and RUSSELL L. ADAMS, "Marijuana Use In High School Students," *Diseases of the Central Nervous System* 33 (Sept. 1972): 603–10.

BRECHER, EDWARD M., "Marijuana: The Health Questions," *Consumer Reports* 40 (March 1975): 3.

CARNEY, P. A., M. W. H. TIMMS, and R. D. STEVENSON, "The Social and Psychological Background of Young Drug Abusers in Dublin," *British Journal of Addiction to Alcohol and Other Drugs* 67 (1972): 199–207.

CLARKE, FRANK H., *How Modern Medicines Are Discovered*. Mount Kisco, N.Y.: Future Publishing Co., 1973.

COHEN, SIDNEY, *The Drug Dilemma*. New York: McGraw-Hill, 1969.

Drug Abuse: Escape to Nowhere. Smith, Kline and French Laboratories.

Drug Enforcement Administration, *Drug Enforcement—Drugs of Abuse*. United States Department of Justice, Washington, D.C., Spring 1975.

Drug Use in America: Problems in Perspective. Second Report of the National Commission on Marijuana and Drug Abuse, Washington, D.C., March, 1973.

EARLE, RICHARD, "Protect Your Child Against Drug Abuse," *Reader's Digest* 102 (Feb. 1973): 199–203.

Food and Drug Administration, FDA Consumer Memo, *Self Medication*. DHEW Publication No. (FDA) 73-3025, Washington, D.C., 1973.

GOLD, ROBERT S., WILLIAM H. ZIMMERLI, and WINNEFRED K. AUSTIN, *Comprehensive Bibliography of Existing Literature on Drugs: 1969 to 1974*. Dubuque, Iowa: Kendall/Hunt Publishing, 1975.

HAASTRUP, S. and K. THOMSEN, "The Social Backgrounds of Young Addicts As Elicited in Interviews With Their Parents," *Acta Psychiatrics Scandinavica* 48 (1972): 146–73.

HEMSING, ESTHER D., ed., *Children and Drugs*. Washington, D.C.: Association for Childhood Education International, 1972.

HINDMARCH, IAN, "The Patterns of Drug Abuse Among School Children," *Bulletin on Narcotics* 24 (July-Sept. 1972): 23–26.

McCRACKEN, SAMUEL, "The Drugs of Habit and the Drugs of Belief," *Commentary* 51 (June, 1971): 43–51.

National Institute of Mental Health, *LSD, Some Questions and Answers*. Washington, D.C., 1969.

National Clearinghouse for Drug Abuse Information, *Narcotics, Some Questions and Answers*. Washington, D.C., 1972.

National Clearinghouse for Drug Abuse Information, *Sedatives, Some Questions and Answers*. Washington, D.C., 1971.

National Clearinghouse for Drug Abuse Information, *Stimulants, Some Questions and Answers*. Washington, D.C., 1971.

RILEY, D. N., and B. D. JAMIESON, "Personality Pathology and Student Drug Use: An Empirical Study," *New Zealand Medical Journal* 76 (Oct. 1972): 252–55.

Strategy Council on Drug Abuse, *Federal Strategy for Drug Abuse and Drug Traffic Prevention.* Washington, D.C.: U.S. Government Printing Office, 1974.

The Drug Abuse Survey Project, *Dealing With Drug Abuse: A Report to the Ford Foundation.* New York: The Ford Foundation, 1972.

THORNBURG, HERSCHEL, "The Adolescent and Drugs: An Overview," *Journal of School Health.* American School Health Association, Kent, Ohio, Vol. 43, No. 10, December, 1973.

WHITEHEAD, PAUL C., "Social and Drug Using Backgrounds of Drug Users Seeking Help: Some Implication for Treatment," *International Journal of the Addictions* 8 (1973): 75–82.

WILLIAMS, JOHN B., *Narcotics and Drug Dependence.* Beverly Hills, Calif: Glencoe Press, 1974.

WITTERS, WELDON L., and PATRICIA JONES-WITTERS, *Drugs and Sex.* New York: Macmillan, 1975.

FOOTNOTES (CHAPTER 5)

[1]Frank H. Clarke, *How Modern Medicines Are Discovered* (Mount Kisco, N.Y.: Future Publishing Company, 1973), p. 10.

[2]*Drug Use in America: Problems in Perspective,* Second Report of the National Commission on Marijuana and Drug Abuse, pp. 76–80.

[3]Food and Drug Administration, FDA Consumer Memo, *Self Medication,* Washington, D.C., DHEW Publication No. (FDA) 73-3025.

[4]National Technical Information Service, *A Study of Health Practices and Opinions* (Philadelphia: National Analysts, Inc., 1972), pp. iii–vii.

[5]John B. Williams, *Narcotics and Drug Dependence* (Beverly Hills, Calif: Glencoe Press, 1974), p. 23.

[6]*Ibid.,* p. 282

[7]Samuel McCracken, "The Drugs of Habit and the Drugs of Belief," *Commentary* 51 (June, 1971), p. 44.

[8]The Drug Abuse Survey Project, *Dealing With Drug Abuse: A Report to the Ford Foundation* (New York: The Ford Foundation, 1972), pp. 60–61.

[9]Williams, *op. cit.,* p. 42.

[10]Williams, *op. cit.,* p. 282.

[11]National Clearinghouse for Drug Abuse Information, *Sedatives, Some Questions and Answers,* Washington, D.C., 1972, p. 1.

[12]Williams, *op. cit.,* p. 200.

[13]Weldon L. Witters and Patricia Jones-Witters, *Drugs and Sex* (New York: Macmillan, 1975), p. 256.

[14]Sidney Cohen, *The Drug Dilemma* (New York: McGraw-Hill, 1969), p. 11.

[15]Drug Enforcement Administration, *Drug Enforcement—Drugs of Abuse* (Washington, D.C.: U.S. Department of Justice, Spring 1975), pp. 26–27.

[16]Edward N. Brecher, "Marijuana: The Health Questions," *Consumer Reports* 40, No. 3 (March, 1975), p. 149.

[17]Drug Enforcement Administration, *loc. cit.*

[18]Strategy Council on Drug Abuse, *Federal Strategy For Drug Abuse and Drug Traffic Prevention* (Washington, D.C.: U.S. Government Printing Office, 1974).

[19]Cohen, *op. cit.*, p. 7.

[20]National Institute of Mental Health, *LSD, Some Questions and Answers,* Washington, D.C., 1969, p. 4.

[21]Esther D. Hemsing, ed., *Children and Drugs* (Washington, D.C.: Association for Childhood Education International, 1972), p. 41.

[22]D. N. Riley and B. D. Jamieson, "Personality Pathology and Student Drug Use: An Empirical Study," *New Zealand Medical Journal* 76 (Oct. 1972).

[23]*Ibid.*, p. 400.

[24]Donald E. Barnes and Louisa Messolonghites, *Preventing Drug Abuse* (Boston: Holt, Rinehart and Winston, 1972), p. 4.

[25]P. A. Carney, M. W. H. Timms, and R. D. Stevenson, "The Social and Psychological Background of Young Drug Abusers in Dublin," *British Journal of Addiction to Alcohol and Other Drugs,* 67 (1972), p. 205.

[26]Eduardo Baselga, "Young Drug Users: Sociological Study of One Sample," *Bulletin on Narcotics* 24 (July–Sept. 1972), p. 22.

six

COUNTERMEASURES AGAINST ALCOHOL, TOBACCO, AND DRUG ABUSE

The preceding chapters have attempted to identify pertinent factors relating to the use and abuse of alcohol, tobacco and drugs. This use and abuse have caused untold problems in individual and family anguish, economic waste and societal counterproductivity.

We have discussed the short and long term effects of the use of these drugs on the quality of life, and seen that there is no one reason that people use drugs, but many. If this book stopped at this point, it would not have covered, perhaps, the most important area—what has been and should be done to combat the problems that have resulted from the misuse of these drugs.

The following pages will discuss some of the counter-measures—actions taken in opposition to other actions—that have been tried against the misuse of alcohol, tobacco and drugs. After the successes and failures are identified, some modifications of existing programs as well as new alternative programs will be suggested.

ALCOHOL COUNTERMEASURES

Alcohol use in American society today is accepted as normal behavior. As a result, many people do not see alcohol abuse as a problem. This has been a major reason why countermeasure efforts have been largely unsuccessful.

Alcohol is the most commonly used and abused drug in the United States today. The American people drink for all sorts of reasons—to celebrate; socialize; solve problems; escape; for religious reasons; to dull or lessen bad emotional feelings such as depression, guilt, fear, hate; to accentuate happy feelings; and to lessen physical pain. The reason people begin to drink may not be the same reason they continue to drink, and eventually abuse alcohol. There very rarely is one simple reason for drinking.

Drinking can be called a *syndrome*. A syndrome is a combination of symptoms resulting from multiple causes; it therefore requires a multi-faceted approach to be controlled or arrested. Various rehabilitation programs have been developed all across the nation. But programs will do little good unless they have sufficient economic and manpower resources, and are able to reach all those individuals affected by the problem.

Alcoholics Anonymous. Probably the most well-known program is Alcoholics Anonymous (AA). Because of the heavy reliance on AA, the NCA (National Council on Alcoholism) and the local alcoholism councils have focused less on promoting programs for alcohol abusers than have most other national health and social welfare groups.[1] AA is one of the major therapeutic systems in the field of alcoholism, yet the population attracted to and benefiting most from the organization is primarily middle class. See Chapter 3 for a discussion on the organization and function of AA.

Al-Anon and Alateen. A number of other organizations developed as a result of the success of Alcoholics Anonymous. Al-Anon is an organization of spouses and other relatives of alcoholics. Alateen is a similar organization for the teenage children of an alcoholic parent. The value of membership, of course, is to learn that others have similar problems and to benefit from their insights and experiences. These groups serve a useful adjunct function and support other therapy programs.

Drug Therapy. Some treatment programs for alcoholism utilize drugs to help maintain abstinence or to alleviate feelings that lead to drinking, such as depression. Antabuse (disulfiram) therapy began in the early 1950's and is considered a valuable adjunct in treatment programs. The drug works by sensitizing the alcoholic in such a manner that one drink will cause a dramatic negative reaction.[2] But only infrequently is it effective when used as the primary focus of treatment. In a sense, the helpfulness of drugs in the treatment of alcoholism is as much psychological as pharmacological.

Behavioral Conditioning. There are two general behavioral conditioning techniques in the treatment of alcoholism, one designed to accomplish abstinence (aversion therapy) and one designed for controlled drinking. Both techniques are used more effectively with the more stable patients from the middle and upper classes. Use of either technique requires the understanding of the patient and a willingness to endure discomfort in order to reach a distant goal.

Psychotherapy. Treatment programs utilizing psychotherapy have been quite successful for many individuals, with long-lasting results. To be sure, to treat the alcoholic, the patient's level of social and economic functioning, social class, and depth of psychopathology must be taken into account. The therapist works with individuals, groups and families to help them change their behavior in a more positive direction.

Uniform Alcoholism and Intoxication Act. For several hundred years, public intoxication has been handled under criminal law only. In the 1940's, and in the 1950's, laws were enacted to decriminalize public intoxication, but the effect on alcohol abuses and public authorities did not take place until after 1966. (See section on "Alcoholism as a Disease" in Chapter 3.) As a result of landmark court decisions at that time, much progress has been made toward the medical and rehabilitative treatment of intoxication and alcoholism. There continues to be a need to recognize alcohol abuse as an illness or sickness, and as a developing illness with early warning signals.

Potential Solutions

If allotted the resources, economic and human, to establish a program for alcohol use and abuse awareness, the government should set up a campaign using all media resources (radio, television, and newspapers) to inform and educate the public about alcohol use and abuse. A nationwide mass-media educational program, in order to be successful, should first have its goals and values well-defined. The words "alcoholism" and "addiction" should be defined to avoid misunderstandings. The local definitions and interpretations could be arrived at through value clarification sessions, perhaps through a local parent-teacher organization.

There would, obviously, be quite a wide difference of opinion on the goals and objectives of such a program. For example, should the solution to alcohol abuse be total abstinence or some degree of moderation? Such an educational program would also have political and economic connotations. The alcohol producers would lobby against it. Politicians in jurisdictions that are high in alcohol-producing labor force would object to it.

One approach might be to work the educational program into the existing structure at one uniform grade level. What would happen, for example, if the program were incorporated into the present U.S. public school systems, at one specified grade level, but in *all* schools. All energies in the public schools could be focused in this one area, with thoroughness the objective. In addition, the program could be integrated into each and every community organization and all private educational institutions. To merely educate the student population is inadequate; we also must educate the parents.

All traffic violations involving alcohol should result in immediate, enforced suspension of the license to drive. This action would probably be effective in the case of the social drinker but not the alcoholic; however, even the alcoholic should have his license suspended. This would be practical if the law-enforcement budgets and manpower forces across the U.S. were equal to the needs of the community. Educational centers could then be programmed to work with all violators of this law. Examples of programs would be "Court Schools for Drunken Drivers," "Court Schools for Problem Drinkers," and "Alcohol Safety Action Programs." State and federal prisons and correctional centers should also develop and put into practice alcohol use and abuse educational programs. Television and radio programs for men, women and children could devote a portion of their broadcasting time to alcohol education.

It is imperative that a nation-wide fight against alcohol abuse be put into practice. Program objectives should be to inform the public about the problems concerning alcohol abuse and to modify the present behaviors of alcohol abusers while attempting to create a program that will fit the needs of each and every individual in our society.

Over the long run, most of the care and treatment of alcoholics will have to be provided through basic helping services to be developed in every community. The magnitude of the problem requires that the entire helping structure be mobilized to cope with it; anything less cannot possibly solve the problem. Alcohol problems do not exist in isolation from other social, psychological and health problems, and it will be difficult to devise a system of specialized facilities to deal with the many problems associated with alcoholism. But, does this mean that society should not try?

Prohibition was once used as an approach to solve the problems that alcohol had created in our society. As history has shown, this was not and is still not a feasible solution to our modern-day problem of alcohol abuse, because millions of people want to drink alcoholic beverages in a social setting.

Society cannot close its eyes and pretend not to see the problem as it is. If individuals and groups demand the solution to this problem, our leaders must and will respond. Many of the problems of alcohol abuse can be controlled and be a part of our past. The solution can only come through time, money, manpower and caring.

It is clear that there is a need for the following resources in treating alcohol abuses:

1. inpatient and outpatient services
2. detoxification centers
3. intermediate or transitional services
4. nonmedical emergency services
5. vocational rehabilitation—equipping a person to function in a working capacity

In addition, treatment and rehabilitation programs must be conducted within industrial and military settings. There is a need for physicians to accept and treat alcoholics as "sick" people, *and* hospitals and physicians should stop denying that patients have alcohol problems. Also, individuals need to learn how to encourage a loved one with a drinking problem to go for help.

Education is a primary prevention tool that can counteract alcohol abuse. The Cooperative Commission on the Study of Alcoholism concluded that one way to prevent problem drinkers from developing is to reduce the emotionalism associated with alcoholic beverages. That emotionalism results from, among other things, the following:

1. Continuing disagreement between "drys" and "wets"
2. Residues of the Prohibition experience
3. Differences in attitudes toward alcohol between generations
4. Various symbolic meanings assigned to drinking and abstinence[3]

Another way to prevent potential problems is to educate the public about the responsible use of alcohol. A second special report to the U.S. Congress on *Alcohol and Health* provided some guidelines for the responsible use of alcohol. They are:

1. Make sure that the use of alcohol improves social relationships, rather than impairing or destroying them.
2. Make sure the use of alcohol is an adjunct to an activity rather than being the primary focus of action.
3. Make sure alcohol is used carefully in connection with other drugs.
4. Make sure human dignity is served by the use of alcohol.[4]

Further, one can encourage responsible drinking by others in the following manner:

1. Respect the person who chooses to abstain.
2. Respect the person who chooses to drink in moderation; do not be insistent about "refreshing" his drinks or refilling his glass.
3. Provide food with alcohol at all times, especially proteins such as dairy products, fish, and meats.
4. Provide transportation or overnight accommodations for those unable to drive safely, recognizing that the host is just as responsible for preventing drunken driving as his guests.[5]

The time has come for major program efforts to prevent the abuses of alcohol. We must develop healthy attitudes and drinking patterns toward alcohol for the many members of our society who will inevitably drink.

TOBACCO COUNTERMEASURES

Much publicity has been given recently to the respiratory diseases, especially lung cancer, emphysema, chronic bronchitis and heart disease. Cigarette smoking and, to a lesser extent, pipe and cigar smoking, have been cited as causal factors in respiratory and heart diseases of smokers and of affected nonsmokers. The American Cancer Society, the American Heart Association, the Lung and Tuberculosis Association, state and federal governments, and other agencies and individuals are concerned with helping people eliminate cigarette, cigar and/or pipe smoking as personal practices in their daily living.

Some people are able to stop smoking completely; others are able to cut down on the amount of smoking they do or on the quantity of some harmful substances in their tobacco. Others have been unable, temporarily or permanently, to quit. It is generally acknowledged that people smoke for different reasons—for example, because of peer pressure, to relieve stress or to lose weight. Whatever the reasons for smoking, there have been various suggestions for stopping smoking.

Most experts feel that smoking is a learned practice and that to stop smoking requires that one reverse the learning process.

DeMente lists four qualities he feels one needs to kick the smoking habit permanently: (1) motivation; (2) insight; (3) attitude; and (4) practice.[6]

Many experts agree that the decision to quit must not be a whim but a strong rational decision to benefit one's health and the health of one's family. For learning (the development of the smoking practice) to occur initially, there must be emotional involvement and other reasons. Learning of any behavior occurs through a combination of intellect and emotion, and to change complex smoking behavior also involves both intellect and emotion.

Stopping techniques appeal to the intellect, emotions, social conscience, economic concern, or to any combination of these. When one decides to quit smoking, knowing the reason(s) for beginning the practice may aid the smoker and those involved in helping him to get a better profile of the smoker and their predicament.

The *Smoker's Self-Testing Kit*, developed by Dr. Daniel Horn and members of the staff of the Public Health Service's National Clearinghouse for Smoking and Health, is designed to determine what the smoker knows and feels about smoking. It consists of four tests: the *first* to discover if one really wants to quit smoking; the *second* to find out what the smoker knows about the effects of smoking on health; the *third* to tell what kind of smoker one is—why one smokes; and the *fourth* to tell whether the smoker's environment will help or hinder his or her stopping efforts.[7]

The two basic approaches to help people stop smoking are the *individual* approach and the *group* approach. These are, however, not mutually exclusive. Each individual has the opportunity to choose either approach or a combination of them. Individualized stop-smoking proposals include: (1) individual counseling; (2) hypnosis; (3) the American Heart Association's five-week "How to Stop Smoking" withdrawal program; and (4) the Seventh Day Adventist program, "Five Day Plan."

Whatever the method, the smoker must make two decisions: (1) Can I do without smoking? and (2) What method(s) will I use—cold turkey? tapering off? How will I go about quitting? It is a generally held assumption that beginning smokers will have less difficulty and more success in their endeavors to quit than long-time smokers.

Some individuals have devised their own techniques for stopping smoking. One man found he did not enjoy smoking in the dark. Others find that eliminating coffee helps decrease their smoking, since coffee-drinking and cigarette-smoking often are partners. Some people use oral substitutes for cigarettes—gum, toothpicks, food of various kinds, a rolled-up piece of paper, a pacifier, fingernails (biting them) and pipes and cigars (chewing on them), among others.

Others try action substitutes such as knitting, whittling, painting, and sewing. Still others may set time and space limitations upon themselves, such as smoking only when in a particular room, or smoking only "x" number of cigarettes per week or per day in their attempts to decrease or eliminate their smoking practices.

Group anti-smoking methods have proliferated in the last few years. For example, the National Tuberculosis and Respiratory Disease Association developed an instructional booklet for a student-conducted campaign in high schools. Included are administrative suggestions, projects, contests, displays, questionnaires, and success hints.

Probably the most well-known stop-smoking clinics are: (1) Smoke Watchers; (2) SmokEnders; (3) Seventh-Day Adventists' Five-Day Plan; (4) American Cancer Society; (5) American Heart Association; and (6) National Tuberculosis and Respiratory Disease Association or Lung Association. The last four provide free clinics.

Many experts regard the group cigarette-withdrawal programs as means of helping those who need supportive assistance. Though not noted as an important consideration in most programs, the personality of the smoker may play an important role in determining whether a given program or type of program is worthwhile for that particular individual at that time. DeMente lists and discusses fifteen different methods to stop smoking and a brief review follows.

The Schick Way to Stop Smoking, developed in 1970 at the Schick-Shadel Hospital in Seattle, Washington by Smith and Chapman, is based upon counterconditioning, "a system designed to change the response of the Instinctive Memory and thereby eliminate the urge to smoke."[8] This method employs daily mild electrical shocks, the degree of which is determined by the patient, from electrodes attached to one arm while the person smokes. It also employs one session of "inhalation therapy"—smoking three cigarettes as fast as possible and inhaling ten deep puffs every minute. Reinforcement group sessions are conducted for ten weeks, once a week, after the initial five day period.

SmokEnders' Way to End Smoking, developed by a dentist and his wife, Dr. and Mrs. J. Rogers of eastern Pennsylvania, is a ten-week program based upon behavior modification through positive reinforcement techniques. It was designed to be conducted by the program graduates, former smokers. There are eight specific goals of the system:

To change your life-style from that of a smoker to a nonsmoker;
To instill in you a strong sense of accomplishment and pride;
To eliminate your guilt feelings and increase your sense of self-worth;
To rid you of "smoker's hysteria" (fear of being caught without your cigarettes, the compulsive scramble to borrow, buy or steal a cigarette when you run out, etc.);
To increase your self-confidence;
To re-establish your ability to function at full par without cigarettes;
To provide you with sincere fellowship;
To give you both physical and emotional freedom from an undesirable enslavement.[9]

The morning after the fifth meeting everyone quits smoking. Because the program is based on improving one's self-image and positive feelings about self, the day is, according to the Arizona Program Director, "most often accompanied by a happy, almost euphoric sense of freedom and self-mastery."[10] The organization also publishes a monthly *SmokEnder Newsletter*.

DeMente also discusses transcendental meditation and smoking. He reports that,

in 1973 behavioral scientists reported that from 85 to 95 percent of drug users voluntarily kicked the habit once they got into meditation. The same researchers also report that meditation is equally effective in eliminating dependence on tobacco smoking.[11]

The seven basic steps in the TM course are: (1) a free introductory meeting; (2) a free preparatory lecture; (3) a private interview; simple meditation technique taught; assigned a (confidential) personal mantra; (4)–(7) additional guidance; practice meditating while being observed by the instructor.[12]

The Famous 5-Day Plan was developed by J. Wayne McFarland and E. J. Folkenberg. It is now sponsored by the Seventh Day Adventists Church and the National Health Foundation. In modified forms it is being used by numerous other groups and physicians. The program itself consists of five ninety-minute to two-hour meetings on consecutive nights. The five meetings consist of lectures, discussions, films and literature about smoking and health damage to the body and about kicking the tobacco habit. The ten key points of the rest of the program are:

(1) Drink six to eight glasses of water between meals.
(2) Drink much fruit juice and eat different kinds of fruit.
(3) Take hot and cold or warm and neutral baths morning and night.
(4) Avoid all alcohol or caffeine-containing beverages.
(5) Do physical fitness exercises daily.
(6) Take walks immediately after each meal; do deep breathing exercises while walking.
(7) Stay away from people who smoke; avoid tension-producing situations.
(8) Go to bed one to two hours earlier than usual.
(9) Make entries into a daily control booklet.
(10) Select a "buddy" from others in the group—compare notes, receive and give encouragement.[13]

The American Heart Association's Five-Week Plan was developed by Dr. Donald T. Fredrickson, who calls it the "work cure."[14] The descriptive pamphlet, *How to Stop Smoking*, describing pertinent information and the method employed, is available through local American Heart Association offices.

The "Dear Smoker" System was developed by Dr. Elsie V. King to help the smoker *control* the smoking habit. DeMente reports that it "consists of a series of step-by-step exercises designed to help you develop mastery over your smoking behavior"[15] so that "you will smoke deliberately and deliciously when you choose to smoke. . . . if you choose to quit smoking entirely, you will be able to do so once you have completed the course."[16]

The Orange County (California) Christmas Seal Course is considered to be "one of the most comprehensive smoking cessation programs now available."[17] The program includes two forms: (1) one version, *Breaking Paper Chains: A Guide for Organizing Smoking Cessation Classes*, functions as training for cessation class leaders; (2) *Tobacco Road: A Guideline for High School Smoking Cessation Classes* is "especially designed for young people who 'resist threatening admonishments regarding their smoking' and is based on learning how to do without smoking." It consists of seven sessions over a three-week period of time. The sessions are devoted to four major phases: physiological, psychological, social and implementation considerations.

The National Tuberculosis and Respiratory Disease Association (Lung Association) has published a pamphlet, *Me Quit Smoking? How?*, which provides practical suggestions for stopping smoking. Example suggestions include:

> Learn/practice being a non-smoker.
> Get a friend to quit with you.
> Organize a no-smoking group at work.
> Ask the Association about a smoking clinic.

They also provide suggestions on the personal level similar to those of the Seventh Day Adventists' program.[18]

The Saunders Stop Smoking Guide is a four-week course developed by George M. Saunders in 1969 and promoted by the American Cancer Society. The Saunders technique, "basically a self-help technique practiced in a group environment"[19] includes: (1) a scoring system to determine what kind of smoker one is; (2) a booklet with practical suggestions; and (3) homework assignments to help stop smoking, such as wrapping a pack of cigarettes in a sheet of paper and recording every cigarette smoked on that paper.

DeMente mentions that money can be used to stop smoking. Two examples of using money as a way to persuade oneself to stop smoking are given by the U.S. Department of Health, Education, and Welfare: (1) $1.00 for every cigarette smoked over a set limit; make limit smaller and smaller; at the end of 50 days, quit smoking completely; (2) donate 25 cents to a charity for every cigarette smoked. The basic idea is that the expense will be too great for the smoker to continue smoking for a very long time.[20]

Researchers at Harvard University Medical School designed the *Smoking on Cue* cessation program. "You smoke on cue from a signaling device carried in your pocket or purse." The purpose of this technique is "to eliminate the relationship between the habit and your daily behavior." The researchers found that with nicotine addiction, the reduction of cigarettes (part of their program) tended to stop at 12 to 14 cigarettes per day and not go below that. "The researchers concluded that to be successful, any approach to kicking the tobacco habit would have to include both psychological and physiological techniques."[21]

The Nicotine Satiation Technique is an aversion technique. It is described as follows:

> One of the most successful techniques of "immunizing" the body against smoking was devised by Drs. David P. Schmahl, Edward Lichtenstein, Darrell E. Harris, Gary Buchler and James Wohl of Oregon. In this technique, the person who wants to quit smoking is isolated in a small, enclosed room that is then filled with warm, smoky air or warm mentholated air (whichever you prefer). The person then proceeds to puff away rapidly on one cigarette after another until he or she is thoroughly sick of them.[22]

Researchers N. H. Azrin and J. Powell (Anna State Hospital Behavior Research Laboratory, Anna, Illinois and Southern Illinois University) developed *The Locking Cigarette Case*. The case locks itself automatically for a set period of time after each cigarette is removed. It signals the user when it is time for another cigarette. In effect, this case is supposed to force the smoker to smoke only a limited number of cigarettes per day. The time device can be reset to prolong time periods during which the case is locked.[23]

DeMente also lists twenty-five self-control techniques people have used successfully. Some involve money as a persuader, others include friends and oral substitutes. Some are those suggested by a number of the group cessation programs.[24]

The fifteenth way DeMente proposes is "example, the best persuader," from the Chester County, Pennsylvania schools. He states that "example is still the greatest teacher of all, but the non-smoker has to let the world know he is an example!" The point of the "example" program is to make non-smoking an *act* so it can compete with the act of smoking. As DeMente states, ". . . since non-smoking is a non-action, non-smokers are not naturally conspicuous examples." This program worked to make non-smokers and non-smoking conspicuous.[25]

Other gadgets and methods which are supposed to help one stop smoking include: (1) *Dialing Your Way to Freedom*'s patented "Dial Holder," a "dial" cigarette holder to help smokers reduce the amount of smoke inhaled over a six-week period. At the end of that period of time, the holder should be allowing no smoke through, thereby stopping smoking for the user; (2) *The Smoker's Kit* which consists of four cigarette holders that gradually reduce the amount of tar and nicotine inhaled.[26]

Concerning group techniques and their success, DeMente points out that "individual behavioral changes occur most often in the context of a group, which is why smoking cessation efforts are more often successful when they involve groups of people."[27] However, he does not substantiate his contention with facts and proof or with a functional definition of "success."

Throughout the preceding discussion, little mention has been made of the success of each withdrawal clinic and technique, and for a good reason. According to a 1969 evaluation by Jerome L. Schwartz, former project director for the Smoking Control Research Project, Institute for Health Research, Permanent Medical Group–Kaiser Foundation Health Plan, "standardized criteria for measuring success in smoking cessation programs have not been established."[28]

There is a third approach which has not been explored or used as extensively as the individualized and group approaches—the *mass media*. The potential of the mass media as a positive force in this, and in other health-related endeavors, needs to be investigated and utilized.

Potential Solutions

Society is trying to discourage smoking with group clinics, educational materials, educational programs, solid factual evidence, gimmicks and gadgets, concerned agencies and volunteers. Research studies have shown the effects of smoking on pregnancy, teenagers, children, air pollution and diseases. In addition, there are cigarette label warnings, banning of television cigarette advertising, decreased smoking on television programs, etc. *Analysis of all these efforts toward creating a non-smoking society will reveal that we have not been very successful.* Although there has been a general unwillingness to ban cigarette smoking and a general unwillingness for individuals to ask smokers to not smoke in their presence, there have been some positive steps. The National Tuberculosis and Respiratory Disease Association points to some such advances:

> The 1965 passage of the federal law requiring cigarette packages to carry warning labels; the 1970 law prohibiting television and radio cigarette advertising.
> The 1964 formation of the National Interagency Council on Smoking and Health to spearhead citizen education.
> Establishment of the National Clearinghouse on Smoking and Health.
> Increased research concerning the behavioralistic aspects of smoking.
> Experimental efforts to help people stop smoking.
> Legislation to increase cigarette taxes; more strict enforcement of not selling cigarettes to minors.
> Prohibiting more and more cigarette smoking in public places— schools, libraries, hospitals.
> Increasing amounts of available educational materials.[29]

The Association points to one very important factor in cessation of smoking. They state that ". . . the solution depends on growing numbers of individuals. Cigarette smoking will be curbed only when *they* (WE) come to a firm decision: young people—not to start; adults—to stop."[30]

Some people have begun to take a stand on the smoking issue. Rights of nonsmokers have become important. One person who has become a positive force is the singer, Vicki Carr. She asks her audiences not to smoke while she is performing. We need to make similar declarations and decisions as smokers who will quit and as nonsmokers who will provide peer and/or social pressure to eliminate smoking in our environment.

To this point, the discussion has focused on secondary and tertiary prevention and concerns alerting and aiding those who are already smoking and who are exposed to smokers. What about *primary prevention?*

The Swedish government has set a primary prevention goal of

colossal magnitude for Sweden—"general eradication of smoking in a generation." They plan to start with "one year's crop of live births—just over 100,000 babies—and raise them to adulthood as nonsmokers, continuing the program year after year for a quarter century." They will begin with maternity clinics, midwives, obstetricians, expectant mothers, then follow through their growth process and schools.[31]

Is stopping smoking in the United States important enough for each of us to conduct a similar personal program? Do we see "smokers' rights" as more important than "nonsmokers' rights" and quality of our immediate air?

There is now a rising concern about the health of nonsmokers exposed to "second-hand air." These nonsmokers include fetuses, children in their homes and communities, teenagers in high schools (in the lavatories, in particular), and adults at work and throughout their daily lives.

The nonsmokers' "Bill of Rights" seems to have given courage to some, though not enough, nonsmokers to demand cleaner air. If extensive enough, social pressure and/or peer pressure, especially in the teenaged and adult populations, can have profound positive effects upon preventing smokers from becoming hazardous to nonsmokers. Smokers are now isolated in the back of buses and planes and in separate railway cars, and are prevented from smoking in some public places (though this may not always be maintained in practice). More social pressures are needed to raise smokers' social consciences. Requesting that no one smoke at meetings and conventions is a step in positive social pressure. Will individuals have the courage to take such a stand with friends and acquaintances?

The facts and negative results of smoking have not been effective in deterring smoking. The economics of smoking have not halted smoking. Can social stigmatization be the force to stop smoking in our culture?

Techniques are available for those who actually decide to quit smoking. It is hoped that one of the techniques described will be successful. We must implement primary prevention programs to eliminate smokers. But there are thousands, perhaps millions of people who do not want to stop smoking. What can be done to halt their practice, which is affecting not only their own health but the health of those around them? Do individuals in this independent society have a responsibility toward each other person or only toward themselves? Does the welfare of the total society need to be considered as paramount in the smoking–nonsmoking struggle? When will society determine to stand firmly on the question of smoking so that all may benefit in their daily lives?

DRUG ABUSE COUNTERMEASURES

When America decided it had a drug crisis, the result was a haphazard public campaign against drug misuse. Agencies, organizations, commissions, committees, etc., were set up. Laws were proposed, passed, or toughened. Conferences were held, speeches made and films produced. Articles, books, pamphlets, and other literature were published. Despite the public crusade against drug abuse, the United States still has a drug problem—and there does not seem to be much evidence to indicate that the situation is improving.

Drug Legislation

Drug abuse has been recognized as a major national health problem and it has become a criminal law problem of frustrating magnitude. Most of the drug legislation has been ineffective and somewhat ambiguous. It has been difficult for the laws to take into consideration the complexity of the drug habit because of the many variables such as type of drug, the quantity used, frequency of use, means of administration, elimination rate, chemical response, and tolerance of the user.

During the 1850's and 1860's, Chinese laborers introduced opium smoking in the United States. San Francisco adopted an ordinance prohibiting opium smoking in 1875. This ordinance was a form of racial hostility against the Chinese, rather than health-oriented. Other cities and states soon followed San Francisco's example and passed similar laws.[32] When the laws failed to serve their purpose, Congress intervened and a series of laws prohibiting importation of smoking opium resulted—and did not solve the problem. During the many years of city, state, and federal efforts to suppress opium smoking, the amount smoked per year increased sevenfold—without taking into account smuggled supplies. Even as late as 1930, opium smoking dens could be found throughout the nation.[33]

It is well-known that morphine use prevailed during Civil War times and the opiates were standard ingredients in various patent medicines. From 1865 to 1900 addiction to narcotics in general was widespread, as was documented in an early survey.[34] In the early 1900's legislative bodies passed laws concerning the use and sale of marijuana and opium.[35]

The Pure Food and Drug Act of 1906 made it mandatory that the label on a patent medicine state if it contains opiates or certain other drugs. In a subsequent amendment, the quantity of each drug was also required to be stated on the label. Other amendments set up standards of drug identity and purity which had to be met. In a way, the 1906 act helped to protect addicts, and along with educational campaigns against these patent medicines, the act helped to curb the making of new addicts. In fact, there was a modest decline in opiate addiction until 1914.[36]

In 1914, Congress passed the Harrison Narcotic Act which stipulated that anyone engaged in the production or distribution of narcotics must register with the federal government and keep records of all transactions. It also provided that all drug handlers pay a tax; therefore, enforcement would reside with the Treasury Department. It further provided that unregistered persons could buy drugs only upon prescription of a physician, for *legal medical use.*

From 1920 to 1933, another drug, alcohol, was banned in the United States, but people continued to consume large quantities of it anyway.

> If nothing else, Prohibition taught us that when respect for a law is gone, then the power of that law is also gone.[37]

Or, as Duster puts it,

> . . . laws which attempt to change the existing moral order are doomed to failure.[38]

It has been said that the harmful effects of alcohol are greater and far more prevalent than those of other addictive drugs; however, literature and the news media do not show this to be the general belief. Furthermore, possession of alcohol is not illegal, as it is for other drugs. Just before prohibition of alcohol was repealed, prohibition of drugs began. The Uniform Narcotic Act of 1932 dealt with legal limitations of the manufacture, transfer, sale, use and possession of "narcotic"* drugs. Since the Act made possession of marijuana illegal and studies of it were discouraged, this law restricted research so that little could be done to find out what marijuana actually is and does.[39]

After World War II, the U.S. was confronted with abuse of yet another group of chemical substances (glue, amphetamines, barbiturates)—some never heard of before (LSD, Speed).

More recently, when it was discovered that abuse of drugs, particularly hallucinogens, seemed to be increasing, some advocated decriminalization of the possession or use of certain drugs, and some asked for tougher laws and enforcement, especially against the suppliers. Interestingly, the harsher the laws and enforcement against drug suppliers, the higher the street prices of drugs and the higher the value and/or amount of stolen goods (higher crime rate). It is ironic that by trying to eliminate addiction almost exclusively through legal means, society has created a thriving black market which is sustained by crime.

Why the Law has Failed.   It appears then, that the laws have for the most part failed as a countermeasure against drugs. Why have they failed? First, because drugs are addicting—physically and/or psychologically. Drug legislators have erred in assuming that addicts can stop taking narcotics anytime they want to and that fear of imprisonment will motivate all types of drug abusers to stop.

Second, because of black market economics. The risks involved in drug traffic are outweighed by the lure of high profits. Tactics are simply changed to find new ways of distribution and new customers in order to maintain those profits.

Another reason for failure is that drug legislation is directed to a moral area which is private (willing sellers and buyers) and victimless (no plaintiff). Other laws similarly aimed at moral change, such as gambling and sex acts, have likewise had little effect in behavioral change.

Lastly, a general lack of respect for the law has been created because of the harshness of the drug laws, particularly in regard to marijuana.

*Narcotic is in quotes because it also includes marijuana, which is not a narcotic.

What Should be Done. On the international level, efforts should be continued to achieve worldwide cooperation in stopping the flow of dangerous drugs into the black market. On the national level, laws should be revised and based upon the effect the drug has on the body. Incarceration of drug users should be waived in lieu of treatment and rehabilitation. Emphasis should be placed on the illegal sale rather than possession and use. State laws may differ from the federal laws, and the drug laws and penalties may and do vary greatly from state to state. The state laws are the ones that count, and whatever Congress does will not change these laws. However, what action Congress does take will indicate its attitude and may influence the states.

Alaska and Oregon have passed similar laws legalizing the possession of marijuana for private use in the home.[40] Hopefully, statistics will be carefully kept and the rest of the nation will wait to see what effect this law will have before following suit.

Medical Treatment and Rehabilitation

Throughout the history of public controls, the laws governing drugs have depended largely on the character of the abuser. As long as drug abuse was confined to social or cultural minorities or marginal communities, public awareness and concern were minimal. Now that middle-class youth are involved, a crisis of another kind has been created. Strangely enough, the concern is not so much for the physical effects of the drugs, but rather for the issues of moral change. Drug abuse is seen as an attack on conventional social life. The controversy continues; do we assume a tough attitude (legal) or tender attitude (therapeutic) toward drug users?

America's doctors have been partly responsible for drug problems for several reasons: (1) irresponsible use of addicting and dangerous drugs; (2) abuse of prescribing privileges; (3) error in acclaiming drugs (such as morphine and heroin) as nonaddicting before adequately testing and researching them; (4) failure to comprehend that addiction is pathological so that it could be encompassed by the Hippocratic Oath.[41]

From 1912 to 1924 opiate clinics were in operation to care for addicts while law-enforcement agencies concentrated on curtailing opiate sales. For the most part, the clinics did a good job, and yet they were rejected. But the New York City clinic was a complete failure and came under heavy attack; and the other clinics suffered for it. An important point to bring out in the case of the New York City clinic is that it was actually a detoxification rather than a maintenance clinic; in addition, it was hurriedly set up, understaffed, uninformed, had poorly qualified personnel, and made mistakes in dispensation and dosage of opiates. But just how extensive was the mismanagement and how much good did the clinics accomplish? The clinics were closed before these questions could be answered.[42]

There have been and are various intervention programs for treatment of drug addicts. The different approaches include: (1) medical–psychological; (2) legal intervention; (3) community-based; (4) communal; and (5) pharmacotherapy.

Medical–Psychological Approach. The medical–psychological approach assumes that the drug user has a psychological and physiological disorder. He is treated in a hospital setting where he undergoes diagnosis, detoxification or stabilization, and then psychotherapy. For the small percentage of patients whose abuse is related to specific psychiatric disorders, this approach seems to be effective. However, the patients have difficulty in sustaining the motivation for seeking treatment and in effecting change because therapy is long-term and the pleasures derived from drug-taking are immediate. Many respond and behave well in the hospital only to revert to their former ways when they leave. Not only is this method ineffective in a great majority of cases, it is also expensive.[43]

Legal Intervention. Legal intervention deals on one hand with various forms of incarceration. This method of confining the drug abuser does not significantly prevent his return to drugs, nor does it alter a criminal way of life.

On the other hand, legal intervention deals with noninstitutional controls such as probation and parole, where the drug abuser volunteers to submit to a treatment and rehabilitation program, periodic checks, avoidance of known drug users and dealers, a regular job, etc. He must fulfill these conditions or be subject to incarceration. The threat of incarceration does keep drug abusers from dropping out of therapy programs.[44]

Community Based Approach. The community-based approach involves treatment focused at changing the individual within his community rather than in institutional isolation. Emphasis is on the practical aspects of daily living. Combinations of various methods are utilized, including counseling, group therapy, vocational training and job placement, pharmacotherapy, and half-way houses. These types of programs are not costly as compared to institutional programs. The community-based approach seems to be most effective when a certain amount of coercion is used because the abuser generally lacks motivation to participate in the program except during time of crisis.[45]

Communal Approach. The communal approach is similar to the community-based but narrower in scope. Emphasis is on mutual support and aid, continual catharsis and confession, and the concept of recovery, but no cure. Examples of such programs are: Synanon, Hilltop, and Phoenix House (24-hour); Reality House (day-care); and Alcoholics Anonymous (frequent meetings). These programs have a better-than-average rate of success and are not costly.[46]

Pharmacotherapy Approach. The pharmacotherapy approach is twofold—maintenance and utilization of chemical antagonists. Chemical antagonists are generally given orally and must be taken regularly, but are not addicting; therefore, cooperation of the addict is needed, or coercion may be necessary. Some antagonists, such as cyclazoncine or naloxone, block the "high" and other pleasurable effects of narcotics; other antagonists, such as disulfiram for alcohol addiction cause an unpleasant reaction when the drug is consumed.[47]

At first glance, chemical antagonists may appear to be the panacea for drug addiction; however, they do have some drawbacks. First, they do not relieve the anxiety, depression, and craving that goes on for months or even years. Also, multiple drug users are a problem, and single drug addicts will shift to another drug. Finally, the side effects and long-term consequences of using chemical antagonists are largely unknown.

The pharmacotherapy approach emphasizing methadone maintenance has probably been the most controversial and may be the most successful of all programs. The majority of methadone programs are mainly concerned with reducing crime and helping addicts readapt to society. Basically what methadone does is block the effects of heroin. It is a narcotic and by definition, addicting. This is not a disadvantage; on the contrary, because it is addicting its continued use will be assured. When methadone is injected, a "high" or effects similar to that of heroin may be experienced. However, when methadone is taken orally, there is no experience of a "high" or other pleasurable effect. It is fully effective for 24 hours when taken by mouth and is dispensed in a hard-to-inject soft drink or tablet form. Once stabilized, the methadone patient is content to remain on the same dosage (or can be reduced).

Brecher reports that:

> An even longer acting drug related to methadone—acetylalphamethadol—is said to be effective for three days or longer and may ultimately replace methadone as a maintenance drug.[48]

Other approaches to help the drug user, employed by numerous local institutions throughout the U.S., include hotlines, rap centers and crashpads; crisis intervention centers; free clinics; and comprehensive drug centers.

Why Medicine Has Failed. Each of the approaches mentioned for the treatment of drug addicts has met with a certain degree of success, but each has also been ineffective for a significant number of individuals. There is relatively little accurate information available to predict which program would be most suitable for a given individual. We must devise a system of keeping accurate statistics if we are ever to evaluate the success of these programs and eventually make a decision on the best way of dealing with the problem.

What about the rise in abuse of licit drugs (tranquilizers, barbiturates, amphetamines) used singly or in combination? Are pharmaceutical companies and doctors guilty of promoting the spread of drug-taking in society? "In 1969, . . . there were 202 million prescriptions for psychoactive drugs prescribed to a population of 200 million. Of these, 80 million were new prescriptions, and these figures do not include prescriptions written in hospitals and clinics . . ."[49]

It is our opinion that many doctors tend to hand out prescriptions for these drugs quite freely. One example that comes to mind is when there is a death in the family. The doctor prescribes tranquilizers, etc., for the surviving spouse (or other relatives) who in many cases really do not need them, but take any comfort that comes along. Instead of one prescription, refills may be prescribed. It is amazing and appalling to see the number of various pills being offered and passed around at some funerals. It also seems to be a common practice to ask patients when they make their sundry complaints, "Do you want 'something' to help you sleep?" or "Do you think you need 'something' to help calm your 'nerves'?"

Our medical schools must step up their programs teaching doctors to recognize drug addiction, especially alcoholism, and they must educate doctors to be more selective in prescribing medicines. Also, physicians should become familier with treatment modalities for drug dependence.

What Should be Done. The federal government supports numerous drug programs with a considerable expenditure of public funds. Millions of dollars are being wasted because these programs are uncoordinated and sadly needing coordinated leadership. Congress should carefully evaluate the total federal drug bureaucracy, and unify and condense it in order to make it more efficient and responsive. Congress should also enlist the aid of experts in the field to assess the scope, incidence and prevalence of the drug problem, and to advise them on the real issues, results and direction.

Drug dependency is extremely complex, involving the interaction of pharmacological, psychological, and social factors; therefore, individual responses to therapy are so varied that no one means of intervention is effective for all drug abusers. The treatment and rehabilitation programs should be coordinated and combined and placed under more medical than political control. There should be a central placement bureau to determine the type of treatment and rehabilitation program or combination of programs best suited to each individual. Emphasis, however, should be placed on methadone maintenance supplied by organized clinics in each state. Whatever the shortcomings of methadone maintenance or other drug treatment and rehabilitation programs, they are by far preferable to the existing black market.

Research in drugs (especially marijuana) should be coordinated, standardized, and encouraged.

The nation's physicians should be called upon to exercise restraint in prescribing potentially dangerous licit drugs; pharmaceutical company cooperation is also needed. The government is placing tighter controls on Valium, Librium, Tranxene and Serax (tranquilizers);Dalmane (sedative), and Clonopin (anticonvulsant). Previously, there was no limit to refills or the life of the prescription. Now, prescriptions can be made only for up to six-months' supply and all handlers must keep careful records.

EDUCATION

Legal controls have been used to try to deter the sale and use of certain drugs by coercion; medical controls have been used to try to terminate drug abuse by various methods of treatment. Both of these countermeasures, have, for the most part, failed. Consequently, as a last resort, in the mid-1960's, America turned to education as yet another form of control, with the primary focus on prevention. It is interesting to note that instead of calling upon all public institutions for cooperation in dealing with the drug problem, one method after another has been implemented in a trial-and-error game. This aimless tack creates pressure for immediate results against great odds. It can also result in a considerable amount of criticism of existing efforts and in opposition to future proposals and programs.

When drug abuse education was formally introduced in the schools, the prevailing theme was to provide students with information about drugs. This approach has been ineffective, because the mistake has been made of equating information with education. The fundamental reasoning behind teaching merely the facts has been that if students know about drugs, their effects, and the laws governing them, they will abstain from using such substances in order to avoid the consequences.

> . . . a major study of New York City prevention programs . . . (1972) found no evidence of any significant relationship between knowledge about drugs or awareness of the dangers of drugs and their actual use. A similar conclusion was reached by a large Pennsylvania Department of Health study in 1970. A Dallas, Texas survey of drug education programs in 1971 suggested that the only significant change in student behavior after a drug education course was increased consumption of alcohol.[50]

It has also been suggested that the presentation of facts alone might prompt students to infer that drugs do provide pleasure and can be used at little risk. Findings by Stuart and Shuman (1972) and Swisher, Crawford, Goldstein and Yura indicate ". . . that a relatively high level of knowledge about drugs is associated with higher levels of drug use.[51] Stuart reports that:

> . . . subjects receiving drug education significantly increased their knowledge about drugs, their use of alcohol, marijuana, and L.S.D., and their sale of the latter two drugs, while their worry about drugs decreased. Neither format nor content factors were shown to influence the results of the program. When the interaction among drug use, knowledge, and worry was examined, it was shown that use tends to rise as a function of the combination of increased knowledge and reduced worry. This combination of factors was not sufficient as a predictor of drug use, however, suggesting the influence of other untested factors. Within the limitations posed by several qualifications it is suggested that these findings support the notion that drug education may not necessarily be positive in its effects, indicating the need for precise measures of program outcomes.[52]

Why Education Has Failed. Why has the dispensation of facts about drugs proved to be a virtual failure? With all the concentrated efforts in drug education, program evaluation was unsubstantial. Few states required any evaluation at all. Of all the countless programs studied by the National Commission on Marijuana and Drug Abuse, not one could be found with an adequate evaluation procedure which could justify its efforts. Those states which did require some evaluation were more concerned with the questions of who should teach the subject matter and at what grade levels it should be introduced. If early and proper evaluation of the desired outcomes had been undertaken, perhaps revisions could have been made and the outcomes more successful.

One must also consider the detrimental factor of untrained or poorly trained teachers who were called upon to teach drug education courses. It appears that teacher training was not considered a top priority until after the programs were started and floundering. For example, as late as 1974, over two million dollars of federal funds were appropriated for the training of school personnel in drug education.[53]

A third reason for failure and perhaps the one with the most consequence has been misinformation and distortion of the "facts." The NEA Task Force on Drug Education claims that not so much the information, but rather the *mis*information could be a contributing factor to the increase in the drug problem.[54] After reviewing over 300 films, the National Coordinating Council on Drug Education found so many scientific or medical misstatements about drugs and their effects, and so many errors that the Council could barely recommend 13 of the films.[55] Films are not the only source of unauthenticity; verbal messages (unqualified teachers) and written materials are just as guilty. According to a Department of Health, Education and Welfare study, most drug educators regard government education materials as ineffective.[56]

Even when students accept information as valid, they will paradoxically disregard the risks and act to the contrary. Several studies have indicated that students discredit drug information because they do not consider it to be credible and because they feel "official" moral values are being promoted. Also, the information offered may not correspond with that obtained from friends or from personal experience or observation of drug use.

The mass media have contributed to the failure of drug education. The mass media reflect and project the values of society. Furthermore, "the mass media legitimize the topic of drug use by the attention they give to the problem through news and information coverage, as well as through the views of life presented in their dramatic and fictional forms."[57] Starting in the sixties an overabundance of news coverage was given to "the drug crisis," which was notably exaggerated and sensationalized. Young people were told that drug abuse was rampant in the schools; which no doubt triggered many nonusers to think, "Oh? I'm supposed to be using drugs? Well, O.K., why not?" and gave rise to an increase in new users. Commercials and ads for patent medicines and other commodities (such as soft drinks) convey the message, "Feel lousy? Take this substance and feel good!" Movies, television, music, magazines, etc., have all reinforced this message.

Finally, a glance at the results of research into the effects of drugs. The "facts" seem to keep changing (for example, in the case of marijuana). In many cases research has been inhibited or prohibited. Statements of fact have been made and then refuted.

What Should Be Done. Since present drug education programs induce a certain amount of use, should efforts in education be continued or scrapped? We believe that trying to prevent through education is by far preferable to trying to cure through treatment and rehabilitation or trying to deter through laws. If methods are failing to accomplish the desired results, they must be carefully evaluated, applied, reevaluated and re-applied, and then altered. Drug education is not only a responsibility of the schools, but also of churches, businesses, physicians and the community as a whole.

Drug education should be part of a regular health education curriculum in kindergarten through twelfth grade, and it should be integrated in other courses such as general science, biology and social sciences. Since drug problems as well as life situations vary from place to place, one drug education curriculum will not suffice for all localities. Before a school devises a drug curriculum a study of their particular situation must be undertaken and then emphasis placed on those areas where help is needed. Further, to be effective, the concentration should be not only on drugs themselves, but on attitudes and conditions that promote drug abuse, and on the individual who abuses drugs.

Drug education must be made relevant to the youth at whom it is directed; courses must be structured to meet each individual's needs. To do this, not only must information about drugs be given, but the reasons which contribute to abuse must be identified; and values must be fostered which promote responsible decision-making in assessing the consequences associated with abuse. Through a variety of techniques such as role-playing, problem-solving, demonstrations, etc., positive attitudes should be developed toward life and self that (1) regard drugs as useful for one's health, but detrimental if misused, and (2) make drugs unnecessary for escape or excitement. Perhaps the curriculum title should be changed to "Respect for Drugs" or "Chemical Substances and Daily Living."

Teachers must help students recognize that chemical substances are not the answer to personal problems and that advertising of patent medicines can be misleading, biased, or false. It is important, also, to have students recognize that all substances have abuse potential including salt, sugar, aspirin, as well as marijuana.

Depending on the particular school situation, some institutional changes may be well worth pursuing, such as: (1) sanctuaries which involve goal-oriented rap sessions and temporary alternative schools such as special classes, mini-schools, storefront schools, etc.; (2) greater use of nonschool personnel such as doctors, ex-users, ex-addicts, hot-line operators, students as teachers; (3) positive alternatives such as TM, political and economic action groups and some recreation.

SUMMARY

Much has been done in the fields of law, medicine, and education to counter the alcohol, tobacco and drug problem in the United States. Most of the measures used, however, have been haphazard, uncoordinated, and ineffective, and have failed. The problem has been approached in a reversionary manner and countermeasures have not been unified and coordinated.

Although the countermeasures have failed, this does not mean that all the drug laws should be erased from the books, treatment and rehabilitation discontinued, or drug education forgotten. All approaches should be reevaluated, revised, and coordinated. Emphasis should be placed in the following order: prevention through education; by treatment and rehabilitation; and deterrence through the full use of existing laws.

BIBLIOGRAPHY (CHAPTER 6)

BAKER, RICHARD J., "Drug Education: Is it Doing Any Good?" *The Education Digest* 38: (Jan. 1973): 38–40.

BLUM, RICHARD H., and associates, *Drug Dealers—Taking Action.* San Francisco: Jossey-Bass, 1973.

BRECHER, EDWARD M., and the editors of *Consumer Reports, Licit and Illicit Drugs.* Boston: Little, Brown, 1972.

BROTMAN, RICHARD, and FREDERIC SUFFET, "The Concept of Prevention and Its Limitations," *The Annals of the American Academy of Political and Social Sciences* 417 (Jan. 1975): 53–65.

CAHN, SIDNEY, *The Treatment of Alcoholics: An Evaluative Study.* New York: Oxford University Press, 1970.

CASRIEL, DANIEL, *So Fair A House.* Englewood Cliffs, N.J.: Prentice-Hall, 1973.

COLES, ROBERT, JOSEPH H. BRENNER, and DERMOT MEAGHER, *Drugs and Youth.* New York: Liveright, 1970.

DELONE, RICHARD H., "The Ups and Downs of Drug Abuse Education," *Saturday Review* 55 (Dec. 1972): 27–32.

DEMENTE, BOYE, *15 Ways to Kick the Smoking Habit.* Phoenix, Arizona: Phoenix Books, 1974.

DOHERTY, JAMES, "Disulfiram (Antabuse): Chemical Commitment to Abstinence," *Alcohol Health and Research World.* National Institute on Alcohol Abuse and Alcoholism, U.S. Department of Health, Education, and Welfare, Washington, D.C., Spring 1976.

DUSTER, TROY, *The Legislation of Morality.* New York: Free Press. 1970.

GUSFIELD, JOSEPH R., "The (F)Utility of Knowledge?: The Relation of Social Science to Public Policy Toward Drugs," *The Annals of the American Academy of Political and Social Sciences* 417 (Jan. 1975): 1–15.

HAMMOND, PETER G., "Turning Off the Abuse of Drug Information," *Library Journal* 98 (April, 1973): 1337–1341.

HOFFMAN, CHARLOTTE, "OE's Drug Education Program," *American Education* 10 (Dec. 1974): 35–36.

KING, RUFUS, *The Drug Hang Up.* New York: Norton, 1972.

National Institute on Alcohol Abuse and Alcoholism, *Alcohol and Health.* U.S. Department of Health, Education and Welfare, A Second Special Report to the U.S. Congress, Washington, D.C., June 1974.

National Tuberculosis and Respiratory Disease Association, *Breathing—What You Need To Know.* New York, N.Y., 1968.

PLAUT, THOMAS F. A., *Alcohol Problems: A Report to the Nation.* Cooperative Commission on the Study of Alcoholism. New York: Oxford University Press, 1967.

SCHWARTZ, JEROME L., "A Critical Review and Evaluation of Smoking Control Methods," (reprint of) *Public Health Reports* 84 (June 1969): 483–506.

SEEGER, MURRAY, "Rearing Nonsmokers," *The Courier Journal and Times,* Louisville, Ky., (Nov. 2, 1975), p. G-8.

South Bend Tribune, "Alaska OKs Private Use of Marijuana," May 28, 1975.

STUART, RICHARD B., "Teaching Facts About Drugs: Pushing or Prevention," *Journal of Educational Psychology* 66 (April 1974): 189–201.

WYKERT, JOHN, "Review of *Mystification and Drug Misuse* by HENRY L. LENNARD, LEON J. EPSTEIN, et al.," *Transaction* (Jan. 1972): 54.

FOOTNOTES (CHAPTER 6)

[1]Sidney Cahn, *The Treatment of Alcoholics: An Evaluative Study* (New York: Oxford University Press, 1970), p. 193.

[2]James Doherty, "Disulfiram (Antabuse): Chemical Commitment to Abstinence," *Alcohol Health and Research World* (Washington, D.C.: U.S. Department of Health, Education and Welfare, Spring 1976), p. 2.

[3]Thomas Plaut, *Alcohol Problems: A Report to the Nation* (New York: Oxford University Press, 1967), p. 138.

[4]National Institute on Alcohol Abuse and Alcoholism, *Alcohol and Health,* A

Second Special Report to the U.S. Congress (Washington, D.C.: U.S. Department of Health, Education and Welfare, June 1974), p. 164.

[5]*Ibid.*

[6]Boye DeMente, *15 Ways to Kick the Smoking Habit* (Phoenix, Arizona: Phoenix Books, 1974), pp. 46–49.

[7]*Ibid.*, p. 54.

[8]DeMente, *op. cit.*, p. 80.

[9]*Ibid.*, pp. 86–93.

[10]*Ibid.*, p. 87.

[11]*Ibid.*, pp. 94–95.

[12]*Ibid.*, pp. 94–98.

[13]*Ibid.*, p. 99.

[14]*Ibid.*, p. 100.

[15]*Ibid.*, p. 101.

[16]*Ibid.*, p. 100.

[17]*Ibid.*, p. 101.

[18]*Ibid.*, pp. 101–103.

[19]*Ibid.*, p. 103.

[20]*Ibid.*, p. 104.

[21]*Ibid.*, p. 105.

[22]*Ibid.*, pp. 105–106.

[23]*Ibid.*, pp. 106.

[24]*Ibid.*, pp. 107–11.

[25]*Ibid.*, pp. 111–12.

[26]DeMente, *op. cit.*, p. 112.

[27]*Ibid.*

[28]Jerome L. Schwartz, "A Critical Review and Evaluation of Smoking Control Methods," (reprint of) *Public Health Reports* 84 (June, 1969), p. 483.

[29]National Tuberculosis and Respiratory Disease Association, *Breathing, What You Need to Know*, (New York, N.Y., 1968), p. 75.

[30]*Ibid.*

[31]Murray Seeger, "Rearing Nonsmokers," *The Courier Journal and Times* (November 2, 1975), p. G-8.

[32]Edward M. Brecher and the editors of *Consumer Reports, Licit and Illicit Drugs* (Boston: Little, Brown, 1972), p. 42.

[33]*Ibid.*, p. 45.

[34]Troy Duster, *The Legislation of Morality* (New York: Free Press, 1970), p. 8.

[35]Joseph R. Gusfield, "The (F)Utility of Knowledge?: The Relation of Social

Science to Public Policy Toward Drugs," *The Annals of the American Academy of Political and Social Sciences* 417 (Jan. 1975), p. 5.

[36]Brecher, *op. cit.*, p. 47.

[37]Daniel Casriel, *So Fair A House* (Englewood Cliffs, N.J.: Prentice-Hall, 1973), p. 158.

[38]Duster, *op. cit.*, p. 24.

[39]Robert Coles, Joseph H. Brenner, and Dermot Meagher, *Drugs and Youth* (New York: Liveright, 1970), p. 157.

[40]"Alaska Oks Private Use of Marijuana," *South Bend Tribune*, May 28, 1975, p. 16.

[41]Rufus King, *The Drug Hang Up* (New York: Norton, 1972), p. 33.

[42]Brecher, *op. cit.*, p. 117.

[43]Richard H. Blum and associates, *Drug Dealers—Taking Action* (San Francisco: Jossey-Bass, 1973), p. 217.

[44]*Ibid.*, p. 226.

[45]*Ibid.*, p. 227.

[46]*Ibid.*, p. 22.

[47]*Ibid.*, p. 221.

[48]Brecher, *op. cit.*, p. 159.

[49]John Wykert, "Review of *Mystification and Drug Misuse* by Henry L. Lennard, Leon J. Epstein, et al.," *Transaction* 9 (Jan. 1972), p. 54.

[50]Richard H. DeLone, "The Ups and Downs of Drug Abuse Education," *Saturday Review* 55 (Dec, 1972), p. 28.

[51]Richard B. Stuart, "Teaching Facts About Drugs: Pushing or Prevention," *Journal of Educational Psychology* 66 (April 1974), p. 189.

[52]*Ibid.*

[53]Charlotte Hoffman, "OE's Drug Education Program," *American Education* 10 (Dec. 1974), p. 36.

[54]Richard J. Baker, "Drug Education: Is It Doing Any Good?" *The Education Digest* 38 (Jan. 1973), p. 38.

[55]*Ibid.*

[56]Peter G. Hammond, "Turning Off the Abuse of Drug Information," *Library Journal* 98 (April 1973), p. 1337.

[57]Richard Brotman and Frederic Suffet, "The Concept of Prevention and Its Limitations," *The Annals of the American Academy of Political and Social Sciences* 417 (Jan. 1975), p. 54.

INDEX

Abstinence, 15–16, 40
Accidents, alcohol and, 50–54, 59
Al-Anon, 136
Alateen, 136
Alcohol, 2, 3, 25–55, 119 (see also Alcoholism):
  accidents and, 8, 50–54, 59
  availability of, 5
  beer and ales, 26, 27, 28, 38
  blood alcohol concentration, 44–48, 51–54
  central nervous system, effects on, 44, 48–54
  distillation, 25, 29–30
  economy and, 8, 30–32
  emotions, effects on, 54–55
  fermentation, 25, 26–29
  hangovers, 49, 63
  intoxication, 45–48
  metabolism of, 42–44
  patterns of use, 40–42
  rates of consumption, 32–39

Alcohol (cont.):
  sensory perception, effects on, 54
  types of, 25
  wines, 27
  withdrawal symptoms, 16, 55–56, 63, 64, 69
Alcoholic Rehabilitation Act (1967), 58
Alcoholics Anonymous (AA), 71–72, 136
Alcoholism, 55–73 (see also Alcohol):
  cardiac disorders, 66, 68
  countermeasures against, 135–40
  crime and, 8–9
  definition of, 55
  disease concept of, 57–59, 137
  education and, 40, 138–40
  gastrointestinal disorders, 66, 67–68

Alcoholism (*cont.*):
  genetic theories of, 22
  incidence, 6, 7
  legislation, 57, 58, 137
  neurological disorders,
    65–67
  personality trait theory of,
    18, 19
  sociological theories of,
    20–21
  stages of, 59–64
  treatment of, 68–72, 136–40
  types of, 56–57
  withdrawal symptoms,
    55–56, 63, 64, 69
Ales, 28
Alpha alcoholism, 56
Amphetamines, 3, 7, 14, 116
Amytal, 119
Antabuse (disulfiram) therapy,
  136
Aspirin, 3
Automobile accidents, 8,
  50–54, 59
Aversion therapy, 70, 137

Barbiturates, 3, 7, 14, 115,
  119–20
Beers, 26, 28, 38
Benzedrine, 116
Beta alcoholism, 56
Birth control pills, 1–2
Blackouts, 61–62
Blane, Howard T., 19
Blood alcohol concentration,
  44–48, 51–54
Brewing industries, 31–32
Bronchitis, 98

Calories, 43–44
Cancer, 2, 90–95

Carbon monoxide, 83, 84, 86,
  96
Cardiac disorders, alcohol and,
  66, 68
Cardiovascular disease,
  smoking and, 95–97
Central nervous system,
  effects of alcohol on, 44,
  48–54
Chafetz, Morris E., 9
Cigarette smoking (*see*
  Smoking)
Cigar smoking (*see* Smoking)
Cirrhosis of the liver, 67–68
Clarke, Frank, 111
Clonopin, 158
Cocaine, 2, 14, 116, 119
Codeine, 121–22
Coffee, 116, 119
Conditioned learning theory of
  drug abuse, 16–18
Congeners, 28, 49
Consumption rates of alcohol,
  32–39
Conventional health products,
  abuse of, 112–13
Crime, 8–9, 115
Cross-tolerance, 15
Cyclazoncine, 155

Dalmane, 158
Delta alcoholism, 57
Delta-9-tetrahydrocannabinol
  (THC), 123
Depressants, 115, 119–20
Distillation, 25, 29–30
Disulfiram, 136, 155
Divorce rates, 9–10
Drug addiction, defined,
  14–15

Drug dependence, defined, 14
Drug habituation, defined, 15
Drug overdose, 2
Drug use and abuse, 100–131
  characteristics of abusers,
    125–31
  classification of, 115–25
  conditioned learning theory,
    16–18
  countermeasures against,
    150–58
  defined, 2–4
  definition of key terms,
    13–16
  depressants, 115, 119–20
  education and, 4, 158–62
  family unit, effects on, 9–10
  genetic theories, 22
  hallucinogens, 115, 122–25
  individuals, effects on, 4–6
  legislation, 3, 150–53
  narcotics, 6–8, 114, 115,
    151, 152
  over-the-counter drugs,
    110, 111–12
  personality trait theory,
    18–20
  prescription drugs, 110, 111,
    156–57
  psychoanalysis theories, 20
  psychological theories,
    16–20
  society, effects on, 6–9
  sociological theories, 20–22
  stimulants, 115, 116, 119
  treatment and
    rehabilitation, 153–58
  withdrawal symptoms, 121

Early stages of alcoholism,
  60–62

Economy, alcohol and, 8,
  30–32
Education:
  alcohol use and, 40, 138–40
  drug abuse, 4, 158–62
Emotions, effects of alcohol on,
  54–55
Emphysema, 98
Ethyl alcohol (ethanol), 25

Family, effects of drug abuse
  on, 9–10
Fermentation, 25, 26–29
Fetal Alcohol Syndrome, 10
Food, Drug and Cosmetic Act
  (1906), 111
Food and Drug
    Administration, 111,
    112
Fort, Joel, 58
Fortified wines, 28

Gamma alcoholism, 56–57
Gastrointestinal disorders,
    alcohol and, 66, 67–68
Genetic theories of drug abuse,
    22

Hallucinogens, 14, 115,
    122–25
Hangovers, 49, 63
Harrison Narcotic Act (1914),
    151
Hashish, 123
Hashish oil, 123, 124
Heroin, 2, 3, 6, 8, 16, 21,
    120–21
Home production of alcohol,
    25, 36, 38–39
Hydrogen cyanide, 83–84

Inhalation of fumes, 3

Intoxication, 45–48
Isopropyl alcohol, 25

Jellinek, E. M., 56, 58

Korsakoff's psychosis, 65, 67

Later stages of alcohol abuse,
  63–64
Legislation:
  alcoholism and, 57, 58, 137
  drug abuse and, 3, 150–53
Librium, 158
Life expectancy, 88–90
Liver, 42, 67–68
Longevity, 1, 2
LSD, 3, 7, 122–23
Lung cancer, 2, 90–91, 95

Malting, 28
Marijuana, 3, 7, 14, 21,
  123–25, 153
Metabolism of alcohol, 42–44
Methadone, 121, 155–56
Methedrine (speed), 116
Methyl alcohol (wood alcohol),
  25
Middle stages of alcoholism,
  62–63
Moonshine industry, 25, 36,
  38–39
Morning drinking, 63
Morphine, 14, 120, 151
Mortality rates, smoking and,
  88–89
Naloxone, 155
Narcotics, 6–8, 114, 115,
  120–22, 151, 152
Nembutal, 119
Neurological disorders, alcohol
  and, 65–67

Nicotine, 2, 86, 87, 90, 116

Occupation, alcohol use and,
  40–41
Opium, 120, 150–51
Oral cancer, 95
Over-the-counter drugs
  (OTC), 110, 111–12

Pancreatic cancer, 95
Passing out, 61
Patterns of alcohol use, 40–42
Pep pills (*see* Amphetamines)
Personality trait theory of drug
  abuse, 18–20
Physiological therapy,
  alcoholism and, 69–70
Pipe smoking (*see* Smoking)
Pregnancy, smoking and,
  100–101
Prescription drugs, 110, 111,
  156–57
Prohibition, 32, 57, 139, 151
Proprietary drugs (*see*
  Over-the-counter
  drugs)
Psychedelic drugs (*see*
  Hallucinogens)
Psychoanalysis theories of drug
  abuse, 20
Psychological theories of drug
  abuse, 16–20
Psychological therapy,
  alcoholism and, 70
Pure Food and Drug Act
  (1906), 151

Rehabilitation, 4, 8, 153–58
Respiratory diseases, smoking
  and, 98–100, 140–41

Seconal, 119
Sedatives (*see* Barbiturates)
Self-diagnosis, 2, 112, 113
Self-medication, 2, 112, 113
Sensory perception, effects of
    alcohol on, 54
Serax, 158
Smoking, 2, 77–107
    cancer and, 90–95
    cardiovascular disease and,
        95–97
    cessation of, 104–6, 141–50
    characteristics of smokers,
        103
    countermeasures against,
        140–50
    economic cost of, 6
    first smoke, 101–2
    human body, effects on,
        78–88
    pregnancy and, 100–101
    psychology of, 101–4
    respiratory diseases and,
        98–100, 140–41
    statistics on, 88–90
    stress and, 104
Sociological theories of drug
    abuse, 20–22
Sociological therapy,
    alcoholism and, 70

Spiritual therapy, alcoholism
    and, 70
Stimulants, 115, 116, 119
Stomach cancer, 95

Tar, 83, 86, 90, 91
Tea, 116, 119
Tobacco (*see* Smoking)
Tolerance, 15, 47–48, 121
Tranquilizers, 1, 119, 157, 158
Transcendental meditation,
    smoking and, 144
Tranxene, 158
Treatment:
    of alcoholism, 68–72, 136–40
    of drug abuse, 153–58
Tuinal, 119

Uniform Alcoholism and
        Intoxication Act, 137
Uniform Narcotic Act (1932),
        152

Valium, 158

Wernicke's disease, 65, 67
Wines, 27
Withdrawal symptoms:
    alcohol, 16, 55–56, 63, 64, 69
    heroin, 121